Subtropical Gardens

David Bramwell
Zoë I. Bramwell

Editorial Rueda

Porto Cristo, 13 (Parque Lisboa)
28924 Alcorcón (Madrid)

Tel. (91) 619 27 79 • Fax (91) 610 28 55

A Zoë Irene Bramwell

Pages: 4, 26, 32 (Constance Goddard)

I.S.B.N.: 84-7207-086-7

Depósito Legal: M - 37590 - 1995

Imprime: T. Gráfica
Avda. Gumersindo Llorente, s/n
28022 Madrid

Contents

Jacaranda ovalifolia, Constance Goddard (1995)

Preface

This book first appeared as three separate volumes published between 1983 and 1985 under the collective title of "Jardines de Canarias". It is based on the wide spectrum of tropical and subtropical plants to be found growing in the gardens of the Canary Islands and was originally produced as an introductory guide for residents and visitors to the islands to help them identify the species occurring in parks, hotel surroundings and even in private gardens.

The present version, adapted for subtropical and tropical regions in general, was inspired by the large number of requests received by both authors and publishers for copies of the three volumes. These came from people in many parts of the world, from a British Consul in Rangoon to a city garden in Orlando, and demonstrated the interest that the book has for areas other than the Canaries.

I hope that this edition, under the title of Subtropical Gardens will help, therefore, to fill an obvious gap in the literature and aid the plant lovers amongst the many thousands of tourists and travellers who visit subtropical and tropical countries each year, to identify the most common and spectacular garden plants to be found in many of the warmer parts of the world.

Finally, I would like to thank the many friends who have helped to prepare this new edition, in partcular Pilar Echevarría, Alfonso Luezas and Rafael Rueda.

David Bramwell

Introduction

This book provides a basic guide to the most frequent ornamental plants to be found in the parks and gardens of the tropical and subtropical regions of the world extending aproximately between 35° North and South of the Equator. These regions include large parts of Africa, Southern Asia, Arabia, Australasia, the Caribbean, the Canary Islands and Madeira, and the American continent from Argentina to Florida and California. It even extends to the southern limits of Europe especially southern Spain, the French Riviera and the South of Italy.

Within the gardens of these regions there are many historical influences from Islam in southern Asia, North Africa and Spain, the Aztecs in Central America and Mexico, the Spanish colonial influence throughout South America and the Imperial gardens of the British Empire designed to create shade for those "mad dogs and Englishmen" who went "out in the mid-day sun" or at least to enable them to take their afternoon tea in reasonable comfort.

ORNAMENTAL PLANTS

Early in his history, Man discovered how to cultivate plants for his own use and to change from being a hunter-gatherer to a farmer. With the spread of civilization he began to carry seeds, bulbs and cuttings with him to new places and started to alter the natural landscape around his settlements and use plants ornamentally.

The expansion of sea exploration from the fifteenth century onwards opened up new horizons and transported plants over vast distances well beyond their natural capacity for dispersion. This epoch saw the arrival in Europe of ornamental and specially useful species such as potato, tomato, peppers and maize, plants which changed the entire nature of Mediterranean rural economy and cuisine.

The garden flora of subtropical and tropical regions now has its origins all over the world. From the Orient have come such favourites as *Hibiscus rosa-sinensis* and *Thunbergia grandiflora,* Australia has contributed *Acacia (Mimosas),* the beautiful bottlebrush trees *(Callistemon)* and the ubiquitous *Eucalyptus.* The floras of tropical and southern Africa have given us the bird of paradise flower *(Strelitzia)*, African tulip tree *(Spathodea campanulata)* and *Dombeya* from the island of Madagascar. It is, however the American continent which has been the principal source of ornamental species with plants such as the *Jacaranda* and *Passiflora,* from South America, the wax flowers *(Plumeria spp)* from central America and the Caribbean and *Parkinsonia* from the desert of California, all this in addition to the whole Bromeliad family and the Cactaceae.

Amongst the most spectacular of subtropical garden plants are, however, the palms and orchids and these have their origins throughout the tropics and subtropics of the world.

USEFUL PLANTS

Even the most humble plants, apparently with no use whatsoever, play an important role in maintaining the conditions for life on our planet. The oxygen we breathe is a by-product of photosynthesis and plants also control the natural water cycle and soil production, all contributing a habitable, healthy planet.

Although about 90% of the world's food requirements come from less than 20 species of plants, Man uses an enormous number of other species for food, flavourings, medicines, fibres etc. Many of these combine usefulness with ornamental value and are grown for both purposes. Some have remained in gardens as decorative species long after their original use has been replaced by new products.

Amongst the most widespread of the cultivated species are the banana *(Musa spp)*, pawpaw *(Carica papaya),* castor-oil *(Ricinus communis)* and pine-apple *(Ananas comosus).*

SUCCULENT PLANTS

A major group of semi-desert plants which have become an important element of the ornamental garden flora are the succulent plants. These usually survive periods of drought by storing water in their stems or leaves which have become specially thickened and adapted for this purpose. Such adaptations make for unusual plant architecture and permit succulents including cacti to be used as the basis for spectacular displays in gardens fortunate enough to be located where such plants can be grown out of doors.

About 9-10000 species can be considered as succulents and most come from the desert fringes of South and East Africa, southern Arabia, western India and Madagascar or from the southern states of the USA, Mexico, the dry slopes of the Andes and other semi-desert areas of South America. The cacti (Cactaceae) are almost exclusively confined to the American continent whereas their old world counterparts, the *Euphorbia* and *Stapeliads,* are mostly African. Specially rich areas of the world for succulents are the Karroo and Cape regions of South Africa, Madagascar, the East African highlands and the Canary Islands. In the New World, they include Arizona, Mexico and the Andean slopes of Peru, Ecuador and Chile as well as Brazil and Argentina.

GARDENS OF THE CANARY ISLANDS

The Canary Islands due to their geographical location became, from the 15th century onwards, a hub at the centre of new continental trade routes to the Orient, Australia, South and east Africa and the Americas and the importance of their position and their equable subtropical climate is reflected in the present-day Canarian garden flora which has its origins in tropical and subtropical regions throughout the world. Plants of economic value have been introduced into the islands over a long period of time, form the early Spanish settlement of the Islands and later particularly from the exploration of South and Tropical America. Many were first grown and established in the Jardín de Aclimatación Botanical Garden on Tenerife and others were cultivated as curiosities, for their exotic fruit or for their medicinal properties in private gardens such as Las Magnolias in Tafira and Huerta de las Flores in Agaete, both on Gran Canaria. Important collections of cacti and succulents can be seen in the Jardín Canario "Viera y Clavijo" along with a display of native Canarian plants and in Palmitos Park both on Gran Canaria. There are also private but visitable collections at San Nicolas (Gran Canaria) and Adeje (Tenerife) and the island of Lanzarote has a magnificent cactus garden at Guatisa designed by the internationally famous artist Caesar Manrique.

In the Canaries there are a number of public parks and gardens full of interesting exotic species, these include the gardens of Puerto Rico and Arucas (Gran Canaria) and the municipal Parque Garcia Sanabria in Santa Cruz de Tenerife.

Garden design and planning

Tropical and subtropical plants offer enormous possibilities for garden design. Amongst their most valuable features are their wide range of brilliant, bright flower colours, luxuriant growth and the wealth of exotic forms and shapes of fruits and flowers. To make the best use of a potential garden site it is, however, necessary to take into consideration various additional aspects, not just the plants.

Garden design and planning can often bring out undiscovered creative instincts and many of the most attractive gardens have been created by people with very little experience or training. Good powers of observation and a sense of knowing what you want combined with a certain ability to vizualize the "finished" product are the most important factors for success.

If natural features such as rocks, changes in levels and mature trees are present on the garden site these should be incorporated into the design whenever possible as this can save many construction headaches and years of waiting for new trees to mature. Every effort should also be made to use local materials especially if a "natural" effect is required, stone rather than brick and wood rather than artificial materials are generally much more pleasing to the eye even though, at times, they are more laborious and costly to maintain.

The subtropical and tropical climate is conducive to outside living and this provides the oportunity to use terraces and verandahs to convert the garden into an open-air extension of the house. In such circumstances the provision of space for recreation, enjoyment and relaxation is part of the secret of garden design.

For outdoor living shade is an important consideration and flowering trees and climbers can be used to provide protection from the

fierce sun. Pergolas with passion flowers and bignonias can be used to create shady walks and patios. Often a green hedge can be used to give a cool sensation and is much better at reducing glare than a stone or whitewashed wall.

Every garden needs focal points and features and these can be readily created using plants such as palms, yuccas, pandans, evergreen shubs and variegated foliage plants. The trunks of trees and pergola supports can be effectively decorated in an artistic and innovative way using epiphytes such as orchids, ferns and bromeliads.

The art of good garden construction comes from the harmonious arrangement of the various elements. Both the living plants and inert natural materials such as stone and water contribute to the three-dimensional effect fundamental to an artistic balance in the finished product. Water, in particular, can be used to provide both soothing sound effects and a sense of coolness in an otherwise hot and

often overwhelming climate and even the smallest water feature is an essential element of the subtropical or tropical garden. Pools, cascades and small streams add considerable interest to a garden and, especially in dry regions, can be a focal point for bird-life, butterflies, frogs etc.

Subtropical and tropical plants, especially the trees and shrubs, are generally too exhuberant to be confined in formal gardens with regular shapes and straight lines. They are usually better displayed using long, flowing curves and changes in levels. Garden limits and fences should, if possible, be hidden to create an illusion of size so that it becomes difficult to discern, when standing at any one point in the garden, where it begins and ends. The most attractive designs for small gardens, particularly informal ones, foster this perspective of infinite depth and hidden boundaries to give the feeling that the garden is a small part of a much larger one. If the design achieves this then an interesting garden results.

Subtropical gardens with their pergolas, patios, swimming pools and recreational areas often make use of containers and container-grown plants. Containers made from materials such as terracotta, bamboo or even cement come in a great variety of shapes and forms and can add considerable interest to a garden. They are particularly valuable for patio gardens in arid regions where a balance between the need to water sparingly and the desire to have at least a few well-grown specimen shrubs can be achieved by growing cacti, succulents or flowering shrubs such as *Hibiscus* or *Bougainvillea* in large pots or containers.

Soil is a key factor in all gardens but can be vital to their success or failure in hot climates. Tropical and subtropical soils tend to be thin and rather poor and need enriching. Many are volcanic soils with a high mineral content but as these are usually poor in organic material they are easily leached and rendered almost useless by excessive watering. In such cases organic material such as peat, leaf-mould or natural manure should be incorporated annually if the quality of plant-growth is not to be seriously handicapped.

Design and construction are unending processes. The garden changes from season to season and from year to year as trees and shrubs grow and modify their shape in a process that is never finished. New ideas occur and new features and plants require incorporation and give endless pleasure to the gardener in all regions but in few parts of the world are the colourful displays of flowering trees and climbers so delightful as in the tropical garden.

Contents

18

Scientific name	Family	Page
Euphorbia horrida	*Euphorbiaceae*	139
Euphorbia neriifolia	*Euphorbiaceae*	140
Euphorbia pulcherrima	*Euphorbiaceae*	141
Euphorbia resinifera	*Euphorbiaceae*	142
Euphorbia splendens	*Euphorbiaceae*	143
Leonitis leonorus	*Labiatae*	144
Phlomis fruticosa	*Labiatae*	145
Rosmarinus officinalis	*Labiatae*	146
Acacia cyanophylla	*Leguminosae*	147
Acacia decurrens	*Leguminosae*	148
Acacia farnesiana	*Leguminosae*	149
Acacia karroo	*Leguminosae*	150
Acacia longifolia	*Leguminosae*	151
Albizia julibrissin	*Leguminosae*	152
Albizia lophantha	*Leguminosae*	153
Bauhinia blakeana	*Leguminosae*	154
Bauhinia tomentosa	*Leguminosae*	155
Bauhinia variegata	*Leguminosae*	156
Caesalpinia gilliesii	*Leguminosae*	157
Caesalpinia pulcherrima	*Leguminosae*	158
Caesalpinia sepiaria	*Leguminosae*	159
Caesalpinia spinosa	*Leguminosae*	160
Calliandra surinamensis	*Leguminosae*	161
Cassia artemisioides	*Leguminosae*	162
Cassia didymobotrya	*Leguminosae*	163
Cassia spectabilis	*Leguminosae*	164
Ceratona siliqua	*Leguminosae*	165
Clianthus formosus	*Leguminosae*	166
Crotalaria agatifolia	*Leguminosae*	167
Delonix regia	*Leguminosae*	168
Erythrina caffra	*Leguminosae*	169
Erythrina crista-gallii	*Leguminosae*	170
Erythrina lysistemon	*Leguminosae*	171
Gleditsia triacanthos	*Leguminosae*	172

Scientific name	Family	*Page*
Leucaena glauca	*Leguminosae*	173
Parkinsonia aculeata	*Leguminosae*	174
Prosopis juliflora	*Leguminosae*	175
Robinia hispida	*Leguminosae*	176
Robinia pseudo-acacia	*Leguminosae*	177
Tipuana tipu	*Leguminosae*	178
Buddleja madagascariensis	*Loganaceae*	179
Magnolia grandiflora	*Magnoliaceae*	180
Abutilon striatum cv. aureo-maculatum	*Malvaceae*	181
Hibiscus mutabilis	*Malvaceae*	182
Hibiscus rosa-sinensis	*Malvaceae*	183
Hibiscus rosa-sinensis	*Malvaceae*	184
Hibiscus schizopetalus	*Malvaceae*	185
Lagunaria patersonii	*Malvaceae*	186
Malvaviscus arboreus	*Malvaceae*	187
Malvaviscus penduliflorus	*Malvaceae*	188
Thespesia populnea	*Malvaceae*	189
Melia azedarach	*Meliaceae*	190
Artocarpus heterophyllus	*Moraceae*	191
Ficus carica	*Moraceae*	192
Ficus elastica	*Moraceae*	193
Ficus microcarpa	*Moraceae*	194
Morus nigra	*Moraceae*	195
Callistemon rigidus	*Myrtaceae*	196-197
Callistemon viminalis	*Myrtaceae*	196-197
Calothamnus quadrifidus	*Myrtaceae*	198
Eucalyptus lehmannii	*Myrtaceae*	199
Feijoa sellowiana	*Myrtaceae*	200
Leptospermum scoparium	*Myrtaceae*	201
Malaleuca leucodendron	*Myrtaceae*	202
Malaleuca nesophylla	*Myrtaceae*	203
Metrosideros excelsa	*Myrtaceae*	204
Myrtus communis	*Myrtaceae*	205
Psidium cattleianum	*Myrtaceae*	206

Scientific name	Family	Page
Psidium guajava	*Myrtaceae*	207
Syzgium cuminii	*Myrtaceae*	208
Syzgium jambos	*Myrtaceae*	209
Myoporum serratum	*Myoporaceae*	210
Bougainvillea glabra	*Nyctaginaceae*	211
Bougainvillea spectabilis	*Nyctaginaceae*	212
Jasminum polyanthum	*Oleaceae*	213
Fuchsia arborescens	*Onagraceae*	214
Fuchsia triphylla	*Onagraceae*	215
Passiflora X alato-caerulea	*Passifloraceae*	216
Passiflora coccinea	*Passifloraceae*	217
Passiflora edulis	*Passifloraceae*	218
Passiflora ligularis	*Passifloraceae*	219
Passiflora mollissima	*Passifloraceae*	220
Passiflora quadrangularis	*Passifloraceae*	221
Passiflora violacea	*Passifloraceae*	222
Phytolacca dioica	*Phytolaccaceae*	223
Pittosporum tobira	*Pittosporaceae*	224
Pittosporum undulatum	*Pittosporaceae*	225
Antigon leptopus	*Polygonaceae*	226
Coccoloba uvifera	*Polygonaceae*	227
Plumbago capensis	*Plumbaginaceae*	228
Cobaea scandens	*Polemoniaceae*	229
Banksia serrata	*Proteaceae*	230
Grevillea banksii	*Proteaceae*	231
Grevillea robusta	*Proteaceae*	232
Leucospermum cordifolium	*Proteaceae*	233
Macadamia integrifolia	*Proteaceae*	234
Protea cynaroides	*Proteaceae*	235
Stenocarpus sinuatus	*Proteaceae*	236
Punica granatum	*Punicaceae*	237
Amygdalus communis	*Rosaceae*	238
Cydonia oblonga	*Rosaceae*	239
Eriobotrya japonica	*Rosaceae*	240

Scientific name	Family	Page
Prunus persica var. nectarina	*Rosaceae*	241
Coffea arabica	*Rubiaceae*	242
Coprosma repens	*Rubiaceae*	243
Ixora macrothyrsa	*Rubiaceae*	244
Casimiroa edulis	*Rutaceae*	245
Citrus aurantifolia	*Rutaceae*	246
Citrus limon	*Rutaceae*	247
Citrus reticulata	*Rutaceae*	248
Citrus sinensis	*Rutaceae*	249
Simmondsia chinensis	*Simmondsiaceae*	250
Brunsfelsia americana	*Solanaceae*	251
Brunsfelsia calycina	*Solanaceae*	252
Cestrum aurantiacum	*Solanaceae*	253
Cestrum elegans	*Solanaceae*	254
Cestrum nocturnum	*Solanaceae*	255
Cestrum parquii	*Solanaceae*	256
Cyphomandra betacea	*Solanaceae*	257
Datura arborea	*Solanaceae*	258
Datura chlorantha	*Solanaceae*	259
Datura suaveolens	*Solanaceae*	260
Iochroma cyaneum	*Solanaceae*	261
Solandra nitida	*Solanaceae*	262
Solanum jasminoides	*Solanaceae*	263
Solanum muricatum	*Solanaceae*	264
Solanum wendlandii	*Solanaceae*	265
Streptosolen jamesonii	*Solanaceae*	266
Brachychiton acerifolium	*Sterculiaceae*	267
Brachychiton diversifolium	*Sterculiaceae*	268
Dombeya wallichii *(D. X Cayeuxii)*	*Sterculiaceae*	269
Tamarix pentandra	*Tamaricaceae*	270
Citharexylum spinosum	*Verbenaceae*	271
Clerodendron splendens	*Verbenaceae*	272
Duranta repens	*Verbenaceae*	273
Lantana camara	*Verbenaceae*	274

Zantedeschia aethiopica, Constance Goddard (1995)

General Index

INDEX TO COMMON NAMES

Echinopsis eyriesii, Constance Goddard (1995)

Adhatoda vasica

Family: *Acanthaceae*

This very drought resistant shrub originating from Tropical India is a frequent garden plant grown for its white flowers with red markings. The leaf-sap is used as an expectorant and the leaves when boiled with sawdust give a useful yellow dye. The wood produces a very high quality charcoal used in making gunpowder.

Thunbergia grandiflora

Family: *Acanthaceae*

A species originating from the northern region of India. This is a spectacular climber with clusters of large blue flowers with a pale yellow to white tube virtually throughout the year. It is a very rapidly growing plant which rarely sets seed and is quite difficult to propagate from cuttings.

Thunbergia gregori

Family: *Acanthaceae*

From East and South Africa, *T. gregori* is a very useful ground-cover plant producing masses of vivid orange flowers. It can be used as a climber if given suitable support and is excellent for dryish, open conditions. It is usually reproduced from seeds.

Conicosia communis

Family: *Aizoaceae*

A succulent herb with long, linear, fleshy, 3-angled leaves this species is a useful ground-cover plant for dry areas. It has large pale yellow flowers with delicate linear petals. It comes from arid, subtropical regions of South Africa and is uncommon in cultivation. It is propagated by cuttings or seed.

Dorotheanthus bellidiformis

Family: *Aizoaceae*

A herbaceous annual with rough, succulent leaves this species originally comes from the Cape Province of South Africa. Though short-lived, its mass of coloured flowers (red, purple, salmon-pink, yellow, white with coloured tips) make it a most useful ornamental bedding plant in unshaded places. It is normally grown from seed.

Glottiphyllum linguiforme

Family: *Aizoaceae*

Originally from South Africa this yellow-flowered succulent is frequent in cultivation. It has long, tongue-like leaves hence the name *linguiforme* and these are usually soft and glossy-green. Flowering is in Autumn-Winter and the plant requires water during the Winter growing-period. A light, sandy soil is necessary for successful cultivation and propagation is from seed.

Lampranthus spectabilis

Family: *Aizoaceae*

This is a woody-based perennial shrub with long flowering branches and narrow, grey-green, fleshy leaves. The large, very attractive flowers are usually purple, though forms with red flowers such as the illustrated plant are common in horticulture and may be of hybrid origin. The species comes from the Cape region of South Africa and is grown from seed or cuttings.

Trichodiadema densum

Family: *Aizoaceae*

A Cape Province species from South Africa, this plant is an excellent miniature subject for planting amongst rocks or pebbles. Its fleshy roots allow it to survive dry Summer periods and it produces masses of pink-carmine flowers. Once established in a garden it will seed itself into suitable places.

Mangifera indica

Family: *Anacardiaceae*

Over a thousand varieties of this important Tropical fruit are known in cultivation. The «Mango» is of Southern Asian origin and is considered sacred in the Hindu Religion. The orange-red fruit is eaten raw or conserved as jam or when green as chutney. The leaves yield a yellow dye, the wood is employed in India for general construction and all parts of the plant have medicinal uses.

Schinus molle

Family: *Anacardiaceae*

The «Peruvian Mastic» or «California Pepper Tree» is a small tree which is useful as a shade tree or wind break. It is very drought-resistant. The resin from the wood is used as a gum and also as a cure for ulcers as well as for other medicinal purposes. The fruits yield an alcoholic drink in Peru and Mexico and the gum is used for chewing gum.

Schinus terebinthifolius

Family: *Anacardiaceae*

From Brazil, Argentina and Paraguay, the «Christmas Berry» or «Brazilian Pepper Tree» is a very frequently grown tree in Subtropical regions. It is very drought resistant and fast-growing and the leaves are used locally as a tonic. A useful resin known as «Balsamo de Misiones» is extracted from the trunk.

Acokanthera spectabilis

Family: *Apocynaceae*

This South African shrub is commonly grown as a garden plant for its white, strongly scented flowers and black fruits. It is, however, an extremely poisonous plant whose latex, wood and bark are used in parts of Africa to obtain arrow-tip poisons said to be capable of killing a man within one hour. It is grown from seed. The common name is «Winter sweet».

Allamanda cathartica

Family: *Apocynaceae*

The *Allamanda* from Brazil is an attractive, evergreen climbing plant with large yellow flowers. It is most frequently grown as an ornamental and is poisonous but as the name *cathartica* implies an extract of the sap is used medicinally as a cathartic.

Carissa grandiflora

Family: *Apocynaceae*

From the South African regions of Natal and Zululand this thorny, evergreen shrub is known as «Natal plum». It is used for hedging and is also often grown for its ornamental, oval, reddish fruits which can be eaten fresh or made into jellies or pies.

Catharanthus roseus

Family: *Apocynaceae*

This species known as «Madagascar periwinkle» originates from the Indian Ocean island of Madagascar. It was first used as a garden flower but has been found to contain many alkaloids including two of major importance, vinblastine and vincristine, which have been found to be effective in the treatment of some forms of cancer. The plant is now cultivated on a commercial basis in some countries.

Nerium oleander

Family: *Apocynaceae*

The «oleander» or «adelfa» is a Mediterranean species which is widely grown as an ornamental shrub. There are many cultivated varieties with red, pink or white single or double flowers and variegated or green leaves. It is easy to grow, resists drought and wind and survives in coastal conditions. It is, however a poisonous species with many medicinal uses. It is grown from cuttings or seed.

Plumeria alba

Family: *Apocynaceae*

This species probably comes from Mexico and it is known as the «white frangipani» or «West Indian jasmine». It grows best in sheltered, humid conditions and loses its leaves in the dry season. Propagation is usually by means of cuttings taken from the tips of its succulent branches.

Plumeria rubra

Family: *Apocynaceae*

The «frangipani» or «flor de mayo» originates from Central America (Mexico to Ecuador). It has a very strong perfume and is commonly cultivated as a specimen tree. The milky latex has many medicinal uses but is poisonous in large doses. In India it is cultivated in temple gardens and is known as «temple flower».

Thevetia peruviana

Family: *Apocynaceae*

The yellow «oleander» is a very useful garden shrub or small tree originally coming from Tropical America. It is very drought resistant and grows well near the coast. All parts of plant are poisonous but the seeds yield many valuable medicinal products and in the West Indies the plant is important in local folk-medicine.

Brassaia actinophylla

Family: *Araliaceae*

This species, known as the «Australian umbrella tree», is frequently met with in tropical and subtropical gardens where it forms a small tree 9-10 m high. The leaves are very distinctive because of the finger-like lobes and the strange radiating inflorescences give the alternative name of octopus tree. It comes originally from the Queensland area of Australia and usually flowers in early Spring.

Aristolochia gigantea

Family: *Aristolochiaceae*

This extremely spectacular climber comes originally from the tropical forests of Brazil. The giant insect-trapping flowers hang below the vines and have a strong rather unpleasant smell which attracts flies and other insects. In cultivation it rarely produces seeds and usually has to be propagated from cuttings. The common name is «Dutchman's pipe».

Calotropis procera

Family: *Asclepiadaceae*

Usually known as «felt plant» or «crown flower», this species comes from Tropical Africa and India. It has large, stiff leaves and is very drought resistant. The plant has many uses, fibre from the stems can be made into ropes and fishing lines, the floss from the seed pod is used for stuffing pillows and the latex for removing hair from animal hides and for medicinal purposes.

Stapelia leendertziae

Family: *Asclepiadaceae*

A South African species from the Transvaal region, this extremely large-flowered plant is a very attractive and easily grown garden subject. The flowers smell of rotten meat and attract flies for pollination. The species does not tolerate excessive watering and is propagated by means of cuttings or division.

Stapelia flavirostris

Family: *Asclepiadaceae*

A very widespread South African species from Cape Province, *Stapelia flavirostris* is one of the largest flowered species of the genus wih flowers up to 17cm across. It is easily cultivated in dry conditions but rots quickly from the base if overwatered. It is reproduced by rooting individual stems or from seed.

Stapelia semota var lutea

Family: *Asclepiadaceae*

Stapelia semota is an East African species coming from Tanzania The form illustrated is the yellow-flowered one, var. *lutea*. It is rare in cultivation and is only usually found in specialist collections but it grows well in dry, open positions on the rock garden. It is usually propagated by division.

Stapelia variegata

Family: *Asclepiadaceae*

A very commonly cultivated species which comes from Cape Province. S. Africa The large star-shaped flowers smell of rotten and attract flies for pollination. The plant is easily cultivated in pots or in open ground but is very susceptible to over-watering. It is usually propagated by division or by seed.

Stephanotis floribunda

Family: *Asclepiadaceae*

The «wax flower» or «Madagascar jasmine» is a beautiful ornamental climbing plant with highly perfumed, long-lasting white flowers and oval fleshy leaves. It comes from the Indian Ocean island of Madagascar where the white, poisonous latex has minor medicinal value and the flowers are traditionally used for the making of bridal wreathes.

Campsis chinensis

Family: *Bignoniaceae*

This deciduous climber comes from Japan and China, and has large orange red flowers making it a most desirable garden subject. Many hybrids have been produced between this and its smaller-flowered relative *Campsis radicans*. The species may be reproduced from seed and the hybrids usually from cuttings.

Crescentia cujete

Family: *Bignoniaceae*

The «calabash» comes originally from Tropical America and is uncommon in cultivation. The large round fruits are used for ornament or as rattles and the plant has a number of medicinal uses including treatment for snake-bites. The wood is very hard and is used in Mexico for making boats. Propagation is by seed.

Jacaranda ovalifolia

Family: *Bignoniaceae*

The «jacaranda» or «rosewood tree» is one of the most spectacular of all cultivated ornamental trees. It comes originally from dry areas of N. Uruguay, Argentina and Southern Brazil. It is deciduous, producing large clusters of blue-violet flowers before the new leaves and is often planted as avenue tree. Reproduction is from seed.

Pandorea jasminoides

Family: *Bignoniaceae*

An uncommon climbing plant originating from Australia, this species is known as the «bower plant». The flowers are white with a reddish or purple base and are produced in lax terminal panicles and the leaves opposite with 5 –to 9– leaflets. It is normally propagated by cuttings but with difficulty.

Phaedranthus bucinatorius

Family: *Bignoniaceae*

The «Mexican blood-trumpet» is native to Mexico and Central America. It is a very useful plant for covering walls and fences with its spectacular deep-red tubular flowers and evergreen leathery leaves. It is, however, difficult to reproduce as it does not set seed in cultivation and does not grow easily from cuttings.

Podranea ricasoliana

Family: *Bignoniaceae*

A species originating from South Africa this is known as «Port St. John creeper». It is a fast growing climber becoming woody with age. The pink trumpet-shaped flowers are borne in loose panicles and are often striped or mottled with red-purple. It is usually reproduced from seed.

Pyrostegia ignea

Family: *Bignoniaceae*

A very striking, brilliant orange-flowered climber, the «flame vine» comes from Brazil. This species is one of the best garden subjects for subtropical regions. It flowers mainly during Winter and Spring and is a very fast-growing plant which does not, however, produce seed in cultivation and has to be propagated from cuttings.

Spathodea campanulata

Family: *Bignoniaceae*

This very spectacular and well-known tree has several common names, «African or Gabon tulip tree», «African flame tree», «fountain tree», etc., and is frequently seen in avenues and boulevards in tropical and subtropical regions. It is a tree which prefers sheltered conditions and a good water supply and is reproduced from seed or by cuttings. It originates from Tropical Africa.

Tabebuia rosea

Family: *Bignoniaceae*

Variously known as «roble blanco», «zapatero», «white cedar», «trumpet tree» or «West Indian box wood», this tree is a native of the West Indies and Central America. It is a very beautiful flowering tree and its light yellow, hard wood is used for building, furniture and as a substitute for boxwood.

Tecoma garrocha

Family: *Bignoniaceae*

This ornamental subtropical shrub comes from Argentina. It is similar to *T. stans* but differs by its orange reddish flowers and more slender habitat. It goes by the common name of "garrocha" and the roots are used locally in its native country as a source of vermifuge medicine. It can be propagated from seed or by cuttings or layering.

Tecoma stans

Familia: *Bignoniaceae*

«Yellow elder» or «garrocha» is the common name of this American shrub which is found from Mexico to Peru. It is an important ornamental for dry conditions and has been used to produce many attractive hybrids. The roots have medicinal properties and the American Indians made bows from the flexible wood.

Tecomaria capensis

Family: *Bignoniaceae*

A commonly cultivated scrambling shrub known as the «Cape honeysuckle» this plant originates from southern South Africa and is a very useful garden plant for most conditions especially where it can be regularly watered. It can be heavily pruned to improve flowering which is almost all the year round and is grown easily from cuttings or seed.

Chorisa speciosa

Family: *Bombacaceae*

A very beautiful flowering tree coming from Brazil and Argentina *Chorisa speciosa*, «paina de seda», «orchid tree» or «floss-silk tree» is of great ornamental value. The silky hairs surrounding the seeds are used like cotton. The tree is deciduous and the tree is easily distinguished by its spiny trunk.

Cordia sebestena

Family: *Boraginaceae*

West Indian in origin, this very attractive tropical shrub or small tree is known for some reason as the «geiger tree». It has beautiful orange flowers and tolerates relatively dry conditions. It is usually propagated from seed and the sticky fruits are sometimes used for making cough medicine.

Acanthocalycium violaceum

Family: *Cactaceae*

An Argentinian species with very pale violet to white flowers. This plant is one of the few *Acanthocalycium* species to be found frequently in cultivation and is often misnamed as an *Echinopsis*. It requires a dry resting period to ensure flowering and is usually reproduced from seed.

Astrophytum myriostigma

Family: *Cactaceae*

The «bishop's cap» cactus is originally from San Luis Potosí, Tamaulipas and southern Nuevo León in Mexico and was introduced into cultivation in the late 1830's. It is easily grown in full sun and is always propagated from seed as the plants rarely produce offsets. Several forms with 4 or 5 ribs and with more or less intense grey-white markings are known.

Borzicactus icosagonus

Family: *Cactaceae*

The *Borzicactus* all come from S. America, Ecuador, Peru or Northern Chile, *B. icosagonus,* which was discovered by Humboldt, is a native of the Nabon region of Ecuador where it grows on dry hillsides. The orange-red flowers and dense yellow spines make it an interesting plant for arid subtropical gardens.

Cereus peruvianus

Family: *Cactaceae*

The origin of this species is somewhat doubtful, some experts attributing it to Peru and others considerating it to be of hybrid origin. It is widely used as a garden plant in dry regions and is also useful because of its large, globular, red edible fruits. The large white flowers open at night.

Cleistocactus smaragdiflorus

Family: *Cactaceae*

The *Cleistocactus* are so-named because the flowers open very little at their tip. They are usually humming-bird pollinated. *C. smaragdiflorus* is from Northern Argentina and probably also occurs in Paraguay and Uruguay. It is very free-flowering and grows to over 2 m in height.

Cleistocactus straussii

Family: *Cactaceae*

Probably one of the best known of all the cacti, this species has its origin in Bolivia. It is very popular as a house plant as it tolerates cold when kept dry. It is also an excellent plant for the subtropical garden as it is both quick-growing and free flowering. It is easily propagated from seed.

Echinocactus grusonii

Family: *Cactaceae*

The «golden barrel» or «mother-in-law's seat» is one of the most popular cultivated cactus species. It comes from the central region of Mexico and old specimens can reach a diameter of about 1 m. In its natural habit is now an endangered species due to overcollection. It is, however, easily propagated from seed and, in warm conditions, grows quickly.

Echinocereus blanckii

Family: *Cactaceae*

Echinocereus blanckii originates from Northern Mexico and Southern Texas. It is a procumbent plant with rather soft stems which root easily as cuttings. It is eailly cultivated in a sunny position and produces large number of purple flowers about 9-10 cm across in early Spring.

Echinocereus pentalophus

Family: *Cactaceae*

This species comes from Southern Texas and Eastern Mexico. It is a sprawling plant which flowers very freely with large purplish blooms. It is best grown in a rich loamy soil in full sun. Propagation is usually by means of cuttings and it does well as both a garden or greenhouse plant being tolerant of cold temperatures if kept dry.

Echinopsis eyriesii

Family: *Cactaceae*

A very commonly cultivated species with beautiful but short-lived nocturnal trumpet-like flowers. *Echinopsis eyriesii* comes from Uruguay, Southern Brazil and the Province of Entre Ríos in Argentina. It is usually reproduced by rooting the offsets which are produced in large quantities. Many improved colour varieties have been produced by hybridization with other red or yellow flowered *Echinopsis* species.

Espostoa lanata

Family: *Cactaceae*

A south American species from Peru and Ecuador, *Espostoa lanata* is known by most cactus collectors as «Peruvian old man» because of its long white hairs. It is one of the most commonly cultivated cactus species and is used both as an indoor and garden plant. It is usually grown from seed.

Ferocactus glaucescens

Family: *Cactaceae*

This is a globular, glaucous-blue species with yellow spines. It comes originally from Eastern Central Mexico where it is quite rare. In subtropical conditions it is a fast-growing, free-flowering species whose pale yellow flowers produce an abundance of seed. It is a very useful ornamental plant in dry regions.

Ferocactus latispinus

Family: *Cactaceae*

This is a Mexican species which is fairly common in cultivation as it is easily grown from seed, it is a globular, usually unbranched plant. The central spine is very robust and hooked and is said to have been used by the Mexican Indians as a fish hook. The purple flowers remain open for about a week.

Helianthocereus huascha

Family: *Cactaceae*

Originally from Northern Argentina (Yaculata, Catamarca) this is one of the best cactus species for subtropical gardens. It produces masses of flowers and is easly propagated by means of cuttings or division of large, older plants and also grows quickly from seed. A yellow-flowered form is also known and is found occasionally in cultivation.

Hylocereus undatus

Family: *Cactaceae*

This species, commonly called «Honolulu queen» is of unknown origin though it possibly comes from Brazil or from the island of Martinique. It is cultivated throughout the world as a hedge-plant and for its magnificent flowers which open at night and may be up to 25 cm across. The red, scaly fruit is edible when mature.

Mammillaria geminispina var. nivea

Family: *Cactaceae*

This attractive, slow-growing species is found naturally in Central Mexico where it is quite rare. The long white central spines are usually black-tipped and the flowers deep red. The variety *nivea* has very long curved, white spines which may be pink- or red-tipped. Reproduction is by cuttings or more normally seed.

Mammillaria spinosissima var. pretiosa

Family: *Cactaceae*

This is a very variable species from the mountains of Central Mexico near Mexico City. It is a very attractive plant which is quite common in cultivation and various forms exist with white to reddish-brown spines and pink to purplish flowers. These are easy to grow in a well-drained soil and are reproduced by seed or by offsets.

Mammillaria tolimensis

Family: *Cactaceae*

Mammillaria is the largest of all the cactus genera with over 200 species extending from the Southern USA to Colombia and Venezuela. Most species however, are from Mexico which is the home of *M. tolimensis,* an attractive red-flowered species forming large ornamental clumps. It is an excellent plant for rock-gardens and flowers profusely.

Neobuxbaumia polylopha

Family: *Cactaceae*

A very spectacular, pink- to reddish-flowered species
N. polylopha comes from Eastern Mexico and is in
great demand both as a pot and garden plant. It is
relatively fast-growing and sometimes branches from
the base but is susceptible to damage by scale-insects.
Reproduction is always from seed.

Notocactus herteri

Family: *Cactaceae*

This is one of the most decorative of all the *Notocactus* species with its large, deep pink flowers. It comes originally from Cerro Galgo in the Rivera Department of Uruguay and is rather uncommon in cultivation. As it very rarely produces offsets it can normally only be propagated by seed.

Nyctocereus serpentinus

Family: *Cactaceae*

Probably originating from Mexico but possibly also Columbia this species has been in cultivation for many years and was first described as a garden plant in 1801 by Lagasca and Rodríguez. It is a night-flowering species and is known in Mexico as «junco espinoso». It is usually grown from cuttings.

Opuntia microdasy var. rufida

Family: *Cactaceae*

From Northern Mexico and Texas this small shrubby species with reddish-brown, minute spines is frequently grown as a garden plant. It has large yellow blooms and flowers freely in cultivation. White and yellow-spined forms are also common and all three are readily propagated from cuttings.

Opuntia spinosior

Family: *Cactaceae*

One of the cylindrical-stemmed *Opuntia* species often placed in a separate genus *Cylindropuntia* this plant is a native of the Mohave Desert, Arizona, New Mexico and parts of Northern Mexico. It is an attractive red-flowered species which can reach tree-like proportions. It is propagated by cuttings which root very easily.

Opuntia vulgaris var. variegata

Family: *Cactaceae*

Opuntia vulgaris is a very commonly cultivated species coming from Southern Brazil and Argentina. It is fast-growing and flowers freely and is a good garden subject. Individual segments or even young fruit will root easily to form new plants. The variegated form shown here is especially attractive as an ornamental plant.

Trichocereus grandiflorus

Family: *Cactaceae*

Known also as *Helianthocereus grandiflorus* or *Echinopsis rowleyi,* this plant is a native of the Catamarca region of Argentina. It is an excellent garden plant and has also formed the basis for many hybrid forms with double, extra large and multicoloured flowers. It is usually reproduced by offsets.

Trichocereus spachianus

Family: *Cactaceae*

A subtropical species from Western Argentina, *Trichocereus spachianus* is commonly known as the «torch cactus» because of its huge white flowers 20 cm long. The stems grow up to 2 m and the species is a fine garden plant. It can be grown from seed or cuttings and flowers freely.

Lonicera hildebrandiana

Family: *Caprifoliaceae*

This species has the largest flowers of any member of the genus. It comes originally from Burma and Siam and is a rampant climber needing severe pruning whch considerably improves flower production. The flowers are white and gradually fade to a deep orange-yellow.

Lonicera japonica

Family: *Caprifoliaceae*

Native of Japan and probably China, this species is a fragrant-flowered climber particularly for shady areas. The flowers are cream-white on opening but later fade to yellow. In China the bark is used for fibre and the flowers medicinally. The common name is «madreselva».

Carica papaya

Family: *Caricaceae*

The «paw-paw», «papaya» or «melon tree» comes from Tropical South America and the West Indies. The fruit is eaten raw with lime or lemon juice or made into desserts and preserves. It is also used as a vegetable when green. The white latex contains the enzyme papain which is used as a meat tenderizer and for digestive tract medicines. It is normally grown from seed.

Quisqualis indica

Family: *Combretaceae*

A spectacular flowering climber this species, the «Rangoon creeper»is native to South East Asia (Burma, Malaya, New Guinea, Philippines, etc.) and is widely cultivated as an ornamental in tropical and subtropical gardens. The plant enjoys sunny conditions and produces clusters of fragrant flowers which vary from deep red to white. It is used medicinally for worms but in large doses is poisonous.

Cynara scolymus

Family: *Compositae*

This Southern European species has been extensively cultivated since ancient times. It is commonly known as the «globe artichoke» and the fleshy receptacle and young bracts are eaten as a vegetable. The plant is also occasionally grown as an ornamental for its large, bright flowers.

Montanoa bipinnatifida

Family: *Compositae*

Mexico is the original home of the «daisy tree» which is an attractive garden subject as it is a late flowering species (late Summer or Autumn). It requires a sheltered site and should be pruned after flowering in order to improve its shape. It may be propagated by seed or from cuttings taken in the Spring.

Senecio grandifolius

Family: *Compositae*

Originating from Mexico this half-woody shrub is an interesting winter-flowering ornamental species which grows up to 5 m in height. Its flowers are grouped in large golden clusters and are extremely attractive. It needs a damp shady locality and regular watering.

Senecio mikanoides *(S. tamoides)*

Family: *Compositae*

This South African climbers is often known as «German ivy» or «Canary creeper». It is a very common, rampant garden plant which has, in some humid subtropical areas, become a serious weed. It is a useful ground-cover plant with its ivy-like leaves and yellow flowers and is propagated by cuttings or seeds.

Tithonia diversifolia

Family: *Compositae*

A prominent member of the Central American genus *Tithonia,* this commonly cultivated subtropical garden plant has its home in Mexico. Though it is commonly known as the «tree marigold» it is a tall perennial herb, sometimes woody at the base and with large yellow-golden flowers. It flowers very prolifically if well watered and is usually propagated from cuttings though it also sets abundant fertile seed.

Ipomoea cairica

Family: *Convolvulaceae*

Otherwise known as *Ipomoea palmata,* this plant originates from West Tropical Africa, Senegal and Gambia. It is grown widely for its dark-centred purplish flowers and has become naturalized in many places. It is very useful as a cover for fences and walls as well as areas of bare ground. In Hawaii the root sap is used for medicinal purposes.

Ipomoea tuberosa

Family: *Convolvulaceae*

A vigorous climber probably originating from South America, this species is widely cultivated as an ornamental in warm countries. It has bronze, palmate leaves and very desirable yellow tubular flowers which are produced in large numbers in late summer. The woody fruiting heads are often preserved for use in flower-arranging and give the plant its common name «wood rose».

Corynocarpus laevigata

Family: *Corynocarpaceae*

The «New Zealand laurel» or «karaka» is a very useful evergreen tree for coastal regions. The fruits and seeds are eaten locally by the Maoris in New Zealand though the seed, need special treatment as they are poisonous. The wood is also used to make canoes.

Aeonium goochiae

Family: *Crassulaceae*

A local endemic of the Western Canary Island of La Palma, *Aeonium goochiae* is a beautiful pink-flowered species not usually cultivated as a garden plant. It requires a humid, shady locality and is a good subject for rock-walls. It can be grown from seed or cuttings.

Aeonium tabulaeforme

Family: *Crassulaceae*

Aeonium tabulaeforme is a rock-face species from the north coast of the Canary Island of Tenerife where it is locally quite common. It is an interesting garden plant because of its plate-like form but must be grown in a shady place in an almost vertical position. It is usually reproduced from seed.

Cotyledon orbiculata

Family: *Crassulaceae*

A very useful, easily grown garden plant *C. orbiculata* is a Southern African species which occurs from the Cape Peninsula to Angola. It flowers over a long period in Spring and Summer, is reproduced from stem or leaf-cuttings and is drought resistant.

Crassula «Morgan's Pink»

Family: *Crassulaceae*

This plant is of hybrid origin, the parents being *Crassula (Rochea) falcata* and *Crassula mesembryanthemopsis*. It is of special value as a subtropical garden plant as the pink flowers last for a very long time. It is propagated by leaf-cuttings as it does not set viable seed.

Crassula nealeana

Family: *Crassulaceae*

Probably originally from the Cape Province of South Africa, the exact locality of this species remains unknown. It is a very attractive plant and deserves a place in any collection of succulents. It is usually reproduced by means of cuttings which root very easily in dry sand.

Crassula schmidtii

Family: *Crassulaceae*

A very attractive dark-red to carmine-pik flowered succulent perennial which is very good as a ground-cover plant, *Crassula schmidtii* originates from S. W. Africa. Transvaal and Natal. It is a Winter-flowering species which is very easily propagated from leaf-cuttings, stem-cuttings or seed.

Echeveria agavoides

Family: *Crassulaceae*

A Mexican species from San Luis Potosí, this plant closely resembles an *Agave* with its spine leaves. Its orange-pink flowers, however, place it clearly in the genus *Echeveria*. It is a very slow-growing species which flowers profusely in Spring and is usually propagated from seed.

Echeveria derenbergii

Family: *Crassulaceae*

From the State of Oaxaca in Mexico, this species is a marvellous subject for subtropical gardens. Its white-grey rosettes of leaves and orange-yellowish flowers make it most useful for ground-cover or as a specimen rock-garden plant. It is easily propagated from leaf-cuttings.

Echeveria harmsii

Family: *Crassulaceae*

This is a beautiful Mexican species highly prized both by gardeners and the horticultural trade where it has been used as the basis for numerous commercial hybrids such as *E. set-oliver, E. pul-oliver,* etc., which are excellent garden and indoor plants.

Echeveria nodulosa

Family: *Crassulaceae*

A very desirable species for both the garden as an indoor plant because of its pretty pink flowers and red-edged leaves, *Echeveria nodulosa* is from Central Mexico near the city of Oaxaca. It is usually grown from leaf-cuttings rooted by lying them on the surface of dry sand.

Echeveria pilosa

Family: *Crassulaceae*

This is a Mexican species from the ·State of Puebla (Sierra de Mixteca). It is a fine garden plant with its green, pilose leaves and its panicles of orange-red flowers. It can be grown from stem or leaf cuttings or by means of seed. In the garden it requires a shady position.

Kalanchoe laxiflora

Family: *Crassulaceae*

This species originating from the Indian Ocean island of Madagascar is rare in cultivation. The leaves are very variable in shape and colour and a number of forms exist in the natural state. It requires a warm, shady position and is propagated by seed, leaf-cuttings or by adventitious plantlets which occasionally occur along the leaf-margins.

Kalanchoe marmorata

Family: *Crassulaceae*

One of the most common garden succulents, this species is originally from Eritrea and the Abyssinian mountains of East Africa. It is a perennial, branching from the base, with erect or procumbent stems which root with great facility as cuttings. The white flowers are usually produced in Spring.

Kalanchoe pumila

Family: *Crassulaceae*

Kalanchoe pumila is one of a group of dwarf species from the island of Madagascar. Its waxy-grey leaves and contrasting pink-purple flowers make it very popular as a hanging basket plant. It is a tropical species which does not tolerate cold, damp areas and is easily grown from leaf-cuttings.

Rochea falcata

Family: *Crassulaceae*

A species from the South Eastern region of the Cape Province of South Africa, Natal and Barberton, *Rochea falcata* is commonly cultivated for its extremely attractive red flowers and contrasting silvery-leaves. Propagation is by means of stem or leaf-cuttings and seed and *R. falcata* also very valuable as a house-plant.

Arbutus unedo

Family: *Ericaceae*

Known as the «strawberry tree» or «madroño», this species is cultivated as an ornamental and for its edible fruits which are used for making preserves or fermented into an alcoholic drink. The bark is used for tanning and in popular medicine. The species is originally from the West Mediterranean region and reaches Southern Ireland.

Acalypha wilkesiana

Family: *Euphorbiaceae*

The «copper-leaf» or «Jacob's coat» comes from the
Pacific Ocean island of Fiji. It is an important ornamental shrub in Tropical and Subtropical regions
where the variety *macrophylla* is commonly cultivated. The leaves, bark and roots all have medicinal
uses as either diuretics or emetics and in the East
Indies the young, tender leaves are cooked and used
as a vegetable. Reproduction is by cuttings.

Aleurites moluccana

Family: *Euphorbiaceae*

This attractive tree is grown for its fruits which yield candlenut oil and lumbang oil which is used especially for painting wooden boat hulls as a protection against marine boring worms and also for lighting and soap manufacture. The «candlenut-oil tree» comes from Malaysia and the Pacific region where the seeds are eaten after roasting.

Codiaeum variegatum

Family: *Euphorbiaceae*

Commonly known as «croton» this species comes from the S. Pacific from Fiji to Australia. It is grown as an indoor plant in cooler climates and is an important garden plant in Tropical and Subtropical areas. The roots and leaves are used by the people of the Pacific in local medicine and the leaves of some forms are cooked and eaten as a sweet flavouring agent.

Euphorbia cactus

Family: *Euphorbiaceae*

A spiny succulent shrub *Euphorbia cactus* originates from Eritrea and Southern Arabia. It has 3-angled stems and forms plants up to 3 metres in height which are excellent, specimen garden plants. It is usually grown from seed as cuttings are extremely difficult to root.

Euphorbia candelabrum

Family: *Euphorbiaceae*

A rather controversial species with a number of names in different parts of Africa *(Euphorbia ingens, E. ammak,* etc.) *Euphorbia candelabrum* is widespread in dry montane regions from South Africa to Ethiopia. It is an excellent, quick growing garden plant eventually reaching tree dimensions and is usually grown from cuttings.

Euphorbia caput-medusae

Family: *Euphorbiaceae*

This species is from the Cape Province of South Africa and grows in the region of Cape Town. It is a spreading, free-flowering plant which makes an attractive garden subject for rock-gardens and for low borders. It is best grown from seed as cuttings are somewhat difficult to root and may produce rather asymetrical plants.

Euphorbia grandicornis

Family: *Euphorbiaceae*

This species is native to South and East Africa from Natal to Kenya and Tanzania. It is an extremely ornamental, commonly cultivated shrub with wavy-edged stems with paired, long spines. It is rather slow-growing and is propagated from cuttings which also root rather slowly and with difficulty.

Euphorbia horrida

Family: *Euphorbiaceae*

A common species in cultivation both as a pot-plant and in gardens, this plant is a native of the Cape Province of South Africa. It is a very variable species with green and bluish-stemmed forms and white to dark red spines. It is easily grown from seed or from cuttings which must be kept very dry until well rooted.

Euphorbia neriifolia

Family: *Euphorbiaceae*

An arborescent species reaching 5 m in height, *Euphorbia neriifolia* originates from the Konkan and Dekkan regions of Eastern India. The stem is usually 5-angled and the spines dark, almost black. It is a good garden plant especially for dry areas as it requires little water and is usually propagated by cuttings which are best rooted in dry sand.

Euphorbia pulcherrima

Family: *Euphorbiaceae*

One of the most common of all tropical or subtropical ornamental shrubs the «poinsettia», «flor de pascua» or «flor de nochebuena» originates from Southern Mexico. There are numerous cultivars with double bracts, white bracts, etc., and all require ample watering and, after flowering, severe pruning. Reproduction is normally by cuttings.

Euphorbia resinifera

Family: *Euphorbiaceae*

This species is endemic to Western Morocco where it is locally frequent in dry rocky areas. It is quite common in cultivation, both as a pot plant and a garden subject in warm, dry areas. It can be grown from seed or cuttings but is best reproduced by division of larger plants.

Euphorbia splendens

Family: *Euphorbiaceae*

A spiny xerophytic shrub of West Madagascar, this species also goes under the name of *Euphorbia millii*. It flowers throughout the year and is frequently grown as a small garden shrub or indoor plant and is commonly known as «Christ thorn». It is usually propagated by cuttings.

Leonitis leonorus

Familia: *Labiatae*

A very attractive orange-flowered species which comes from South Africa, this is a common species in parks and gardens of tropical and subtropical regions. It flowers from late Summer through to Spring and is usually reproduced by seed. In South Africa it is commonly known as «lion's ears» due to the furry texture of the leaves.

Phlomis fruticosa

Family: *Labiatae*

Commonly known as «Jerusalem sage» this species is native to the Mediterranean region. It is often grown as a garden plant for its attractive yellow flowers and is also used as a pot-herb and as a subtitute for sage *(Salvia officinalis)*. Propagation is by seed and the plant is drought resistant.

Rosmarinus officinalis

Family: *Labiatae*

A Mediterranean shrub, «rosemary» is frequently grown as a herb, the dried leaves used as a flavouring for meat and as an infusion for the relief of asthma. Oil of rosemary (Oleum Rosemarin) is extracted from the leaves and is used in perfume, as a disinfectant and to relieve indigestion. It is an attractive plant which can be clipped into low hedges.

Acacia cyanophylla

Family: *Leguminosae*

This species commonly known as the «blue-leaved wattle» is an ornamental tree from Northern Australia. It is used for forestry in dry areas as it is fast-growing and helps prevent erosion. It is also a useful but short-lived ornamental tree and is normally grown from seed.

Acacia decurrens

Family: *Leguminosae*

The «green wattle» tree, sometimes also called «black wattle», is a fast-growing Australian tree which is extensively used in Subtropical regions for forestry plantations and, in Africa, as a source of firewood. The bark is used in tanning and also produces a form of «gum arabic». The flowers are the «mimosa» of florists.

Acacia farnesiana

Family: *Leguminosae*

This species commonly called the «opoponax» or «sweet acacia» is widely cultivated and naturalized in subtropical and tropical regions. It is originally a native of America and if well pruned forms an attractive small tree with sweetly scented flowers which are used in the perfume industry. It is propagated from seed.

Acacia karroo

Family: *Leguminosae*

A Southern African species often grown as a shade tree the «sweet thorn» or «Karroo thorn» is very useful for dry areas. The leaves are used as fodder and the wood for local building and firewood. The bark is used in tanning and for string and the resin (Cape gum) obtained from the trunk has medicinal properties.

Acacia longifolia

Family: *Leguminosae*

The «golden wattle» comes from South Australia and is one of the most useful species for prevention of soil erosion and stabilization of sand dunes. It is quick-growing and very attractive as a garden shrub or small tree which is easily grown from seed. The Australian Aborigenes are said to eat the seeds in times of drought.

Albizia julibrissin

Family: *Leguminosae*

This is an attractive pink-flowered small tree. It is a native of South West Asia from India to Iran and is usually deciduous. It is resistant to drought and requires a light soil. It is easily grown from seed and is commonly known as «silk tree».

Albizia lophantha

Family: *Leguminosae*

Originally from Australia, this attractive, short-lived shrub or small tree is commonly cultivated as an ornamental for its flowers and foliage. It is, however, very useful for the prevention of soil erosion and the wood can also be used for small ornamental objects. The bark can be used for tanning and is said to have antibiotic properties.

Bauhinia blakeana

Family: *Leguminosae*

«The Hong-Kong orchid tree» was originally thought to be a species from the Far East but it is probably a hybrid of cultivated origin. It does not produce viable seed and has to be propagated by cutting or airlayering. It is, however, well worth growing for its large, scented purple-pink orchid-like flowers.

Bauhinia tomentosa

Family: *Leguminosae*

The «yellow camel's foot» is a small drooping shrub from Tropical Africa, China and India. The flowers are yellow with a dark red spot at the base of each petal and the whole plant is covered with fine hair. It is a delicate plant requiring sheltered, warm conditions and is grown from seed.

Bauhinia variegata

Family: *Leguminosae*

This species, commonly known as the «pink camel's foot» or «ebony wood» comes originally from India. It is a shrub or small tree with beautiful pink flowers and grows best in moist conditions under which it remains evergreen throughout the year. It is normally grown from seed and is quick-growing.

Caesalpinia gilliesii

Family: *Leguminosae*

Commonly known as the «bird of paradise flower» *Caesalpinia gilliesii* comes from Argentina and is one of the most popular cultivated shrubs in subtropical regions. It is easily grown from seed if this is soaked in warm water. It is drought resistant and flowers profusely if grown in rich soil.

Caesalpinia pulcherrima

Family: *Leguminosae*

This very beautiful tropical shrub has many common names, «peacock flowers», «flambo», «Barbados pride», etc. It probably originates in the West Indies and can only be grown in warmer regions where it does best in humid conditions. The plant has a number of medicinal uses and the unripe seeds are eaten in Central America. It is propagated from seed.

Caesalpinia sepiaria

Family: *Leguminosae*

Coming from India this plant is known as «Mysore thorn» or «cats-claw». It is used as hedge plant but has become a troublesome weed in Hawaii. The flowers are attractive and used for leis in Hawaii and the bark is used for tanning in India.

Caesalpinia spinosa

Family: *Leguminosae*

Originally from Western South America this species is commonly known as the «tara». It is a useful small tree which produces yellow flower spikes followed by attractive green-red seed pods which persist for several months. The trunk is spiny and the leaves may fall during dry summer periods. It is grown from seed.

Calliandra surinamensis

Family: *Leguminosae*

Known as the «pink powder puff» this beautiful flowering shrub comes from Surinam. Its wood can be used for carpentry and the bark has many traditional medicinal uses. Some species of *Calliandra* are being planted extensively in tropical and subtropical regions as a local source of firewood.

Cassia artemisioides

Family: *Leguminosae*

The «silver cassia» is an evergreen Australian shrub which is rather rare in cultivation. It is a very attrative garden subject with its silvery leaves and masses of yellow flowers and requires a dry sunny position. It is usually grown from seed and is best pruned after flowering.

Cassia didymobotrya

Family: *Leguminosae*

A tropical African shrub which grows to about three metres, this species is commonly called the «peanut-butter cassia» because of the smell of its flowers. It is easily grown from seed in warm sunny sites and can be pruned to maintain its shape. It is, however, a relatively short-lived shrub.

Cassia spectabilis

Family: *Leguminosae*

A tropical American and West Indian species, this small tree is frequently known as the «popcorn tree» or «yellow shower». It is a most desirable garden plant and forms a very attractive specimen tree. The yellow flowers have a scent resembling violets and are produced in long spikes. It is usually grown from seed or woody cuttings.

Ceratonia siliqua

Family: *Leguminosae*

A Mediterranean tree which is widely cultivated in the Old and New World, the «carob», «St. John's bread or locust bean» is a useful plant. The pods contain 50% sugar and protein and provide a valuable animal food and can also be eaten by humans. The wood and seeds are also used and gum can be extracted from the pods. The seed is used as a coffee substitute.

Clianthus formosus

Family: *Leguminosae*

Though a very attractive and desirable plant the «glory pea» from Australia is rather difficult to cultivate. It is a scrambling subshrub with very striking red flowers with a dark blotch at the base of the petals. It is normally propagated from seed and is best treated as a short-lived perennial. Any seed produced should be kept for propagation.

Crotolaria agatifolia

Family: *Leguminosae*

The «bird flower» is a shub originating from East Africa. It has very attractive large yellow flowers and is very tolerant of dry, hot conditions. It can be grown from seed which must be soaked in hot water before sowing, cuttings or root suckers. The foliage is poisonous to domestic animals.

Delonix regia

Family: *Leguminosae*

One of the most spectacular of all cultivated trees the «flamboyant» is a very rare species from Madagascar. It is also known as «flame tree» or «royal poinciana» and is used as a street and park tree throughout tropical and subtropical regions. It is deciduous in the winter and flowers profusely in early summer. It is grown from seed.

Erythrina caffra

Family: *Leguminosae*

A tall deciduous, spreading tree with thorny branches and trunk. The Erythrinas, usually known as «coral trees», are commonly planted as ornamentals in tropical gardens and their exact identification is sometimes difficult. This species comes from the Cape Province and Natal region of southern Africa. It can be propagated from seed or cuttings.

Erythrina crista-gallii

Family: *Leguminosae*

This is a very attractive, commonly cultivated shrub from Brazil. It is known as the «coral tree» and in Spring produces long, showy inflorescences of red flowers. It is a drought resistant plant but grows best with an ample water supply. It is usually propagated from seeds.

Erythrina lysistemon

Family: *Leguminosae*

A South African species from the Cape region, Natal and the Transvaal, this plant is commonly called the «kaffirboom» or «lucky bean tree». It is a deciduous tree losing its leaves in winter and the flowers appear shortly before the new leaves in Spring. It can be grown from cuttings or seed and will tolerate a dry, sunny position.

Gleditsia triacanthos

Family: *Leguminosae*

The «honey locust» or «sweet bean» is native to the Eastern U.S.A. but widely naturalized in Southern Europe. The beans and pods are sweet and edible and are used as animal feed or fermented to make beer. The leaves are also useful as forage and the hard, durable wood is made into fence-posts as it does not rot.

Leucaena glauca

Family: *Leguminosae*

A common garden shrub or tree, this white-flowered tree is originally native to Tropical South America but is now widely naturalized in tropical regions. The tree has many uses and the pods and seeds are eaten («wild tamarind») and can be used as cattle and goat fodder. It is usually grown from seed.

Parkinsonia aculeata

Family: *Leguminosae*

Originally from dry regions of Tropical America the «Jerusalem thorn» is now a widely cultivated orna-mental tree. Its weeping form and yellow flowers make it a desirable specimen tree. It requires a warm, sunny position and is very drought-resistant but grows very rapidly when given an adequate water supply. It is usually grown from seed.

Prosopis juliflora

Family: *Leguminosae*

The «mesquite» originates from Northen Mexico and the Southern United States. It is a desert shrub which, cultivation, can be grown as a small tree. The small flowers are rich in nectar and the pods are used for animal fodder. It requires a sheltered position as it is rather shallow-rooted and is grown from seed.

Robinia hispida

Family: *Leguminosae*

A small, deciduous shrub from North America this species is known as the «rose acacia» or «locust tree». The pink-mauve flowers are produced in early Spring and the plant is tolerant of dry situations and poor soil and can easily be transplanted. It is usually grow from seed.

Robinia pseudo-acacia

Familia: *Leguminosae*

The «false acacia» or «black locust» tree is a common ornamental tree in Mediterranean and subtropical regions. It will grow in poor, sandy soils and in areas with little rainfall and has become an important shade-producing tree in such areas. It is grown from seed, cuttings or root suckers. It comes originally from the U.S.A.

Tipuana tipu

Family: *Leguminosae*

Originating from Argentina and Bolivia this species (also known as *T. speciosa*) is a very useful ornamental tree for parks and gardens. It is fast growing and has a spreading canopy and is a good shade-tree. It is summer flowering and requires warm conditions with a good water supply. It is reproduced from seed which must be soaked before sowing.

Buddleja madagascariensis

Family: *Loganaceae*

A large, evergreen shrub which, as its name implies, comes from the island of Madagascar. The honey-scented orange flowers appear in Winter and Spring and the plant is an excellent, resistant, garden subject which is easily propagated by cuttings. It requires a sunny position and well-drained soil.

Magnolia grandiflora

Family: *Magnoliaceae*

This magnificent evergreen tree comes from the South East States of America and especially Texas. It can reach, in optimun conditions, a height of 30m. and its cream-white coloured flowers are amongst the largest and most fragrant of the genus. *M. grandiflora* is a slow growing species which is best grown in relatively cool, humid conditions.

Abutilon striatum cv. aureo-maculatum

Family: *Malvaceae*

The genus *Abutilon* consists of about 150 species of which *A. striatum* is one of the most important ornamentals. The yellow-variegated leaves and pendulous orange flowers which are produced throughout the year make it a most valuable garden plant. It originates from Brazil and there are several improved large-flowered forms.

Hibiscus mutabilis

Family: *Malvaceae*

Commonly known as the «tree hollyhock» or «confederate» or «cotton rose» this frequently cultivated shrub comes from China. The flowers open pale white and darken to deep pink during the day giving the alternative name of «blushing hibiscus». It is grown from seed or cuttings and the bark is a source of fibre for string manufacture.

Hibiscus rosa-sinensis

Family: *Malvaceae*

The most commonly cultivated *Hibiscus* species, this shrub originates from China. There are numerous colur variants, red which is the most frequent, yellow, orange and pink as well as semi-double and double flower forms in which the styles are converted into extra petals. The common red form is excellent for hedges in coastal areas and can be heavily pruned to maintain its shape.

Hibiscus rosa-sinensis

Family: *Malvaceae*

The pink-flowered form of *Hibiscus rosa-sinensis* is one of the most attractive variants of the species as the flowers tend to be much larger than the typical red form. It is, however, slower growing and less resistant to dry conditions.

Hibiscus schizopetalus

Family: *Malvaceae*

This is one of the most attractive of all the 200 or so *Hibiscus* species with its dainty penduous flowers and frilled, reflexed petals. It comes originally from Tropical East Africa and though it needs a sheltered site it is reasonably tolerant of salty conditions. It is used extensively in crosses with *H. rosa-sinensis* to produce hybrid, ornamental forms especially on the island of Hawaii.

Lagunaria patersonii

Family: *Malvaceae*

An attractive, evergreen tree from Australia (Queensland) this species is resistant to drought and coastal conditions. The flowers are a delicate pink colour and the hard round seed-pod contains minute, irritant hairs giving the tree its common name of «pica pica». The hard wood is used in Australia for building and the bark produces a useful fibre.

Malvaviscus arboreus

Family: *Malvaceae*

*M*alvaviscus is closely related to the genus *Hibiscus* *M. arboreus,* a scarlet-flowered species is a tall, robust shrub which originates from Mexico where an infusion of it is used medicinally to treat throat infections. The leaves are velvety and somewhat irregular in shape and the flowers erect.

Malvaviscus penduliflorus

Family: *Malvaceae*

Also originating from Mexico this species has much larger, pendulous flowers than *M. arboreus*. It is a very beautiful but somewhat delicate shrub which requires a sheltered, humid position in order to develop properly. The leaves are glabrous and *Hibiscus*-like but tend to fall in hot dry conditions.

Thespesia populnea

Family: *Malvaceae*

A small tree or shrub *Thespesia populnea* («portia tree», «milo» o «mahoe») is probably native in the Tropical East Indies but has become widely naturalized in Tropical Africa and America. The pale yellow flowers last only a single day. The wood is useful and the young leaves are said to be edible. In the Pacific Islands the plant has religious significance and is planted in temple gardens in Tahiti.

Melia azedarach

Family: *Meliaceae*

The «Persian lilac» or «paradise tree» comes from Northern India and China. It is commonly cultivated and is even naturalized in S. USA, Hawaii, Southern Europe and South Africa. It is a very valuable shade tree with many uses. The seeds are used for beads and for obtaining insecticide. The wood is used for musical instruments and the leaves, flowers and bark have medicinal properties. The tree is poisonous to humans, animals and chickens but not to most other birds.

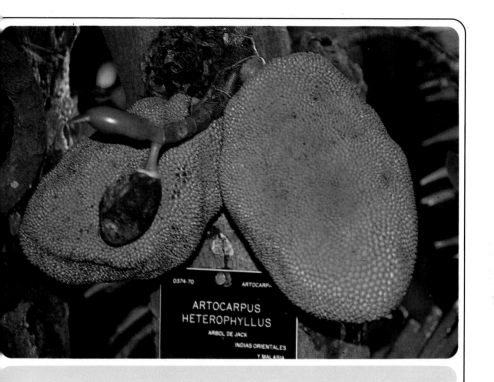

Artocarpus heterophyllus

Family: *Moraceae*

The «jack-fruit» tree is a very useful plant which is native to South India and Malaysia. The wood is excellent for cabinet work and also produces a yellow dye. The pulp and seeds from the enormous fruit are used as food usually boiled in milk, and the leaves provide animal fodder.

Ficus carica

Family: *Moraceae*

The «fig» has been widely cultivated for thousands of years and is naturalized throughout the Mediterranean region. It is a native of South West Asia. The edible fruits are of considerable economic importance and are eaten fresh or made into jams, candies or even an alcoholic drink. A syrup made from the fruits is used medicinally as a laxative.

Ficus elastica

Family: *Moraceae*

Originating from India and Java, the India rubber tree was once a very important source of natural rubber before the discovery of the Brazilian rubber tree *(Hevea* spp.). It is now a very valuable ornamental tree and of considerable commercial importance in temperate regions as an indoor pot plant.

Ficus microcarpa

Family: *Moraceae*

Known as «Indian laurel» or «Malayan banyan» this tropical Asian tree is extensively planted as shade tree in subtropical regions. Its soft wood is used for fire wood and the leaves and bark have many medicinal uses. It is grown from cuttings or by rooting any large piece of branch or trunk but it should not be planted near buildings because of its extensive root system.

Morus nigra

Family: *Moraceae*

The «black mulberry» comes from Iran and South West Asia. It has been long cultivated in the Mediterranean region as a shade tree and for its dark fruits which can be eaten raw or made into preserves. The bark has several local medicinal uses and the leaves can be fed to silk worms.

Callistemon rigidus

Family: *Myrtaceae*

Probably the most commonly cultivated of all the «bottle brushes this species comes originally from dry regions of New South Wales (Australia). It is an evergreen shrub up to 6 m. and is drought resistant. It is reproduced from seed and tolerates quite hard pruning which increases flower production.

Callistemon viminalis

Family: *Myrtaceae*

This is a very attractive, small weeping tree known as the «weeping bottlebrush». It originates from New South Wales in Australia and is a most valued specimen plant. It flowers several times during the year and is best not pruned severely. It is grown from seed or cuttings.

Callistemon rigidus

Callistemon viminalis

Calothamnus quadrifidus

Family: *Myrtaceae*

This is a spreading shrub coming from Western Australia. It is commonly known as «net bush» or «flowering pine» because of its needle-like leaves. It is very drought resistant and is usually grown from seed though it will also root from woody cuttings.

Eucalyptus lehmannii

Family: *Myrtaceae*

This Australian species of *Eucalyptus* is a small tree up to 7 m with attractive flowers and fruits. Like most cultivated *Eucalyptus* the hard wood is useful for general construction and for the paper industry. The leaves and flowers are of medicinal value for treating colds and coughs and as a mild antiseptic.

Feijoa sellowiana

Family: *Myrtaceae*

This small tree originates from South America, Brazil, Paraguay, Uruguay, etc. It is usually cultivated as a fruit tree and is known as «pineapple guava». It is also an attractive ornamental with its white petals and deep red stamens. The leaves are waxy above and densely white-tomentose below. The plant is usually propagated by cuttings.

Leptospermum scoparium

Family: *Myrtaceae*

Commonly known as «the tea tree» or «manuku» this species comes from Australia and New Zealand. It is a good ornamental shrub or small tree and in New Zealand the wood is used by the Maoris for paddles, spears, etc. The bark is used for roofing and the leaves as a substitute for tea.

Melaleuca leucodendron

Family: *Myrtaceae*

The «paper bark tree» is probably of Australian origin but some authorities also suggest New Caledonia or Malaya as its native home. The flowers are pale yellow and some forms have pinkish or purple stamens. It is small tree up to 10 m. and is grown from seed. A medicinal product cajeput oil is extracted from the leaves.

Melaleuca nesophylla

Family: *Myrtaceae*

The «tea-myrtle» comes from Western Australia. It is an attractive mauve-flowered tree and is very drought resistant. Species of *Melaleuca* yield a medicinally useful oil (similar to Eucalyptus oil) on distillation of the leaves and stems and are also very effective for prevention of soil erosion. Propagation is by seed or cuttings.

Metrosideros excelsa

Family: *Myrtaceae*

This beautiful flowering tree comes from New Zealand where it is known as «pohutukawa» or «New Zealand christmas tree». It is very slow growing but provides a valuable timber for boat-making as it is resistant to ship-boring worm (*Teredo* spp.). Infusions of the bark are also used medicinally in its native New Zealand.

Myrtus communis

Family: *Myrtaceae*

The common or Greek «myrtle» is a Mediterranean and West Asian shrub with many mythological and traditional uses. The fruits and leaves are used for flavourings and the leaves were used in religious ceremonies in ancient Egypt, Greece and Rome and in Jewish Festivals. The fruits are medicinal and myrtle oil is an aromatic tonic. The wood is used for furniture, walking sticks and other small items.

Psidium cattleianum

Family: *Myrtaceae*

The «strawberry guava» is from Brazil and Uruguay and is a small, evergreen tree with solitary flowers which are followed by purple, strawberry-flavoured, edible fruits. A yellow-fruited variety var. *lucidum* is very frequently cultivated and the fruits can be made into drinks and jellies or eaten raw.

Psidium guajava

Family: *Myrtaceae*

Known as the «apple guava» or simply «guava» this species originates from Tropical America, West Indies, Mexico and Peru. The white flowers are of ornamental value and the highly fragrant, globose fruits are usually lemon-yellow with white or pink edible flesh which is very rich in vitamin C, iron, calcium and phosphorus. The fruits are eaten fresh or canned.

Syzgium cuminii

Family: *Myrtaceae*

This species is known as the «Java» or «Jambolan plum» and comes from the East Indies and Burma. Though an attractive ornamental, white-flowered shrub it is grown primarily for its purple-black fruits which can be made into wine or vinegar. It grows best in warm, moist conditions and is propagated by seed.

Syzygium jambos

Family: *Myrtaceae*

This species, commonly known as the «Malay-rose-apple» or «Malabar plum» is a native of South East Asia. It is widely grown for its fragrant, edible fruits but its large, cream-white flowers are also extremely decorative. It requires a warm sunny position and is usually grown from seed.

Myoporum serratum

Family: *Myoporaceae*

From Australia and Tasmania this is a most versatile shrub or small tree which is very useful as a hedge plant or wind-break in dry coastal areas. The small purple berries which are much appreciated by birds are also a source of food for the Australian Aborigenes.

Bougainvillea glabra

Family: *Nyctaginaceae*

Originally from Brazil the «bougainvillea» is now one of the most commonly cultivated subtropical plants. This species is the common purple flowered one with glabrous leaves. It can be grown under almost any conditions and is a rampant plant reproduced by cuttings. Pruning improves flower production considerably.

Bougainvillea spectabilis

Family: *Nyctaginaceae*

This species is also from Brazil. It is a much more rampant, less bushy plant than *B. glabra* and is the parent species of numerous colour variants (red, orange, pink, etc.) as well as double forms. It is a drought-tolerant species commonly used for covering walls and fences and can be pruned to form hedges.

Jasminum polyanthum

Family: *Oleaceae*

The «Chinese jasmine» originates from China and probably Japan. It is a very attractive, dainty climber which is most useful for covering wall and fences. It is strongly scented and produces masses of flowers in Spring. Propagation is by root division or by means of cuttings.

Fuchsia arborescens

Family: *Onagraceae*

A Mexican species which is a large shrub bearing panicles of erect, small, lilac-pink flowers. The blue-black berries are also ornamental and the plant is a good subject for sheltered, humid places. It is easily reproduced from cuttings and can also be grown from seeds.

Fuchsia triphylla

Family: *Onagraceae*

This downy-leaved, attractive shrub comes from the West Indies and Haiti. The leaves are usually borne in three's rather than in pairs as in the rest of the genus. The flowers are coral red and the plant has been used as a basis for many cultivated hybrids. It is reproduced by soft wood cuttings.

Passiflora X alato-caerulea

Family: *Passifloraceae*

This is a very attractive, large-flowered hybrid species derived from a cross between *P. alata* and *P. caerulea*. It has large, perfumed pink petals and alternate white sepals. It is reproduced from cuttings or root suckers as it is sterile and does not normally produce fruit.

Passiflora coccinea

Family: *Passifloraceae*

The «red passion flower» is a commonly cultivated ornamental which like the other members of the genus originates from central and southern America. It has large, attractive red flowers and the fruits are edible. This is a very valuable pergola plant which is usually propagated from seed.

Passiflora edulis

Family: *Passifloraceae*

The «purple granadilla» or «parchita» comes from Brazil. It is the most widely grown *Passiflora* species for its edible fruits of which there are two common purple-fruited type and the variety *flavicarpa* which has slightly larger flowers and yellow fruits. Propagation is by seed and growth is very rapid.

Passiflora ligularis

Family: *Passifloraceae*

The «sweet granadilla» or «lemona» is a Tropical American plant which is commonly cultivated for its excellent fruit which can be eaten raw or made into «Batidos». It is usually grown from seed and is a fast-growing plant with considerable ornamental value in warm, humid regions.

Passiflora mollissima

Family: *Passifloraceae*

Commonly known as the «banana passion-fruit» because of its yellow elongate fruit this species is from Tropical America. Its pendulous pink flowers make it an excellent garden subject but it requires a sheltered position as it is easily damaged by wind. It is normally grown from seed and the fruits are edible.

Passiflora quadrangularis

Family: *Passifloraceae*

A species originating from Tropical America this is probably the most spectacular of all the passion-flowers. It is commonly known as the «giant grana-dilla» because of its very large edible fruit. The 4-angled stem is also very distinctive and the leaves are said to have medicinal properties. Reproduction is normally by seeds but is also possible by cuttings.

Passiflora violacea

Familia: *Passifloraceae*

Originally from the Atlantic forests in the Rio de Janeiro region of Brazil, the «violet passion flower» is now a widely cultivated species in subtropical and tropical gardens. It is also sometimes used as an indoor pot plant. Like most passion flowers it is best cultivated on a pergola or against a sunny wall and requires regular watering. It usually propagated from seed or cuttings.

Phytolacca dioica

Family: *Phytolaccaceae*

A large, fast-growing tree from South America the «ombu» or «bella sombra», is an important shade tree in Tropical and Subtropical regions. The wood, though soft, withstands storm and drought. The leaves and shoots are sometimes eaten but contain bitter alkaloids and both the leaves and roots are used medicinally as an emetic and purgative.

Pittosporum tobira

Family: *Pittosporaceae*

A small tree up to 5 m. *Pittosporum tobira* is a common garden plant originally coming from Japan and China. The pale cream flowers are extremely fragrant and appear in early Spring. It is very resistant to drought and is said to be salt-tolerant and so is a useful shrub for coastal regions. A very slow-growing form with variegated leaves is sometimes encountered.

Pittosporum undulatum

Family: *Pittosporaceae*

This Australian species, commonly known as «mock orange», has been cultivated in the Mediterranean region and Subtropical countries for many years. It is easily naturalized due to its sticky, edible, bird-dispersed fruits and its pale greenish-white flowers have a strong scent similar to orange blossom. The species is useful shrub for coastal areas as it is tolerant of salty air.

Antigon leptopus

Family: *Polygonaceae*

A very beautiful climber, this Mexican species is called «coral vine», «Mexican creeper or chain of love». The pink flowers are followed by attractive seed cases making this species a long-lasting ornamental. The giant tubers, up to 7 kilograms, are used as food in Mexico and are said to have a nut-like flavour.

Coccoloba uvifera

Family: *Polygonaceae*

From coastal regions of the American Continent the «sea-grape» or «uva del mar» is a frequently culti-vated street tree in dry subtropical regions. The grape-like fruits are used for wine and gum is made from the bark. The wood produces a red dye and the roots have medicinal value.

Plumbago capensis

Family: *Plumbaginaceae*

A climbing shrub native to the Cape region of Southern Africa, this is a common garden and hedge plant with pale blue or occasionally white flowers. It is poisonous and has some medicinal uses. It requires regular pruning and is best reproduced by means of cuttings.

Cobaea scandens

Family: *Polemoniaceae*

This vigorous climber originates from Mexico and is known, because of the form of the flower, as the «cup and saucer plant». The flower, on opening, is green, later turning to pale mauve and then to deep purple. In Mexico the strange scent attracts bats for pollination. For germination the seeds must be planted erect and not flat to prevent rotting.

Banksia serrata

Family: *Proteaceae*

This species originates from Western Australia. It is a remarkable species with long, erect flowers spikes which last on the shrub for several months. It is easily grown from seed and is fairly drought resistant but grows best on well drained acid soils.

<u>Grevillea banksii</u>

Family: <u>*Proteaceae*</u>

This species, with its brilliant crimson flowers which are produced throughout the year, is a native of Australia. The hairy seed-pods are said to cause severe allergies in some people and are poisonous. The plant needs a protected position away from the wind and is relatively slow growing. Reproduction is from seed.

Grevillea robusta

Family: *Proteaceae*

The «golden pine» or «silky oak» is a large ornamental tree from Australia. It is a fast-growing tree
reachng over 30 m. which produces spectacular
golden yellow flower spikes for several months of the
year. It is resistant to wind but requires ample watering when young. It is normally reproduced from
seed.

Leucospermun cordifolium

Family: *Proteaceae*

From the S.W. Cape region of South Africa, this species is commonly known as the «nodding pincushion». It forms a shrub about 1 m. high and is prized for its flowers which last in water for about one month when cut. It is propagated from seed but is very difficult.

Macadamia integrifolia

Family: *Proteaceae*

The «Queensland nut» originates from Australia. It is a very resistant ornamental tree which produces large quantities of round, brown nuts which have an excellent flavour when eaten raw or roasted. The species is grown commercially in Hawaii and is a potential economic plant. The nuts contain 75% edible oil and the wood is used for furniture.

Protea cynaroides

Family: *Proteaceae*

The «king protea» comes from the Cape region of South Africa. It is a 1-2 m shrub with the flowers grouped into large, attractive cup-like heads with the outer bracts resembling a crown. Propagation is from seed and like all proteas this species can only be cultivated in an extremely well-drained, acid soil with plenty of peat. Proteas should never be allowed to become waterlogged and may die very quickly if they do.

Stenocarpus sinuatus

Family: *Proteaceae*

The «fire-wheel tree» comes from the Australian states of Queensland and New South Wales. It is a spectacular brilliant red flowering tree for lowland humid areas and also yields an excellent dark-brown to reddish hard wood used for furniture and small ornamental objects. It is usually propagated from seed.

Punica granatum

Family: *Punicaceae*

Native to Iran and South West Asia the «pomegranite» is widely naturalized in southern Europe. It is a scarlet-flowered shrub or small tree which yields an attractive edible fruit containing numerous seeds surrounded by sweet, if slightly acid, pulp. Grenadine juice is made from the pulp and the fruit skin is rich in tanin and used in the leather industry. The bark has medicinal uses.

Amygdalus communis

Family: *Rosaceae*

Originally from the East Mediterranean region and Western Asia the «almond» is now very commonly cultivated in S. Europe, N. Africa and in California. The sweet almond seed is eaten ripe, dried or green and can be salted and roasted or made into paste. The bitter almond yields an oil used as a sedative in cough medicine. The kernals of the fruit contain poisonous cyanogenic glucosides.

Cydonia oblonga

Family: *Rosaceae*

The «quince» or «membrillo» is native to Northern Iran and Turkey but is now cultivated in warm temperate and cooler subtropical regions for its large fruits. These are extremely acid and are not eaten raw but cooked to make jam or jelly. The mucilage from the seed is used commercially for making demulcent lotions.

Eriobotrya japonica

Family: *Rosaceae*

Commonly known as the «loquat», «nispero» or «Japanese medlar» this species, though native to China, is very frequently cultivated in Mediterranean and Subtropical regions. The edible fruit is slightly acid and is usually eaten raw or conserved as jelly or jam. It is drought resistant and is used as a pot plant in cooler climates.

Prunus persica var. nectarina

Family: *Rosaceae*

Probably originating in the Far East the «peach» was introduced to Europe by the Romans. There are now many varieties, amongst them var. *nectarina* (var. *nucipersica)* commonly known as the Nectarine. The fruit has a delicate flavour and a smooth, not furry, skin. The stone yields a useful oil and the stem a gum.

Coffea arabica

Family: *Rubiaceae*

Coffee is a shrub which is grown for its seeds which are roasted and ground up to produce the stimulating beverage also called coffee or café. The plant originally comes from the highlands of East Africa but now over 50% of the World's crop is produced by Brazil. The shrub is an attractive ornamental from which home-produced coffee can easily be made.

Coprosma repens

Family: *Rubiaceae*

Called the «mirror plant» because of its glossy leaves this New Zealand species occurs in several variegated forms. Its most common use in cultivation is as an ornamental hedge plant because it is quite drought resistant. *Coprosma* species have a wide range of medicinal uses in New Zealand and form the habitat for rare birds and lizards there.

Ixora macrothyrsa

Family: *Rubiaceae*

Commmonly known as Ixora or «flame bush» this very desirable garden shrub comes from the island of Sumatra from where it was introduced into cultivation in 1878. It has large heads of red-crimson flowers. It requires a warm, lightly shaded site with regular watering and is usually (like most cultivated Ixoras) propagated from cuttings.

Casimiroa edulis

Family: *Rutaceae*

From Mexico and Central America, the «white sapote» is a small tree which produces an edible fruit. The aromatic, fleshy pulp is eaten raw or used in soft drinks. Propagation is usually from seed and there is considerable variation in fruit quality. The seeds are said to have a sedative effect.

Citrus aurantifolia

Family: *Rutaceae*

The «lime» was brought from India to the Mediterranean region by the Arabs over 1000 years ago and is now widely cultivated in tropical and subtropical regions. It is very important for the extraction of lime juice which is rich in vitamin C. Oil of lime is also extracted from the fruit and used in perfume and as a flavouring.

Citrus limon

Family: *Rutaceae*

Also probably coming from subtropical Asia the «lemon» was cultivated by the Greeks and Romans and is now an important economic plant. The juice is rich in vitamin C and B, as well as carotene and contains 5% citric acid which is extracted commercially. Lemon oil and lemon juice are also important products and the latter is a common flavouring for drinks and fish dishes.

Citrus reticulata

Family: *Rutaceae*

This excellent fruit tree, the «mandarin orange», comes from China and is extensively grown in S. Europe and S. United States of America. The same species is the source of related cultivars such as the tangerine and satsuma. As well as being a popular fruit the mandarin yields an oil which is used in flavourings and liqueurs.

Citrus sinensis

Family: *Rutaceae*

The orange originates from China and is probably the best-known of all subtropical fruits. It is rich in vitamin C and is especially important commercially in Spain, South Africa and California. There are many different cultivars but most are rather susceptible to insect pests and need careful cultivation. The peel gives an important oil with uses in perfume manufacture and in medicine.

Simmondsia chinensis

Family: *Simmondsiaceae*

The «jojoba», which comes from California and Mexico, is a desert plant which has, over the last few years, become an important source of liquid wax (jojoba oil) for use as a non-drying lubricant and as base for cosmetic products. It is almost identical to sperm whale oil and its use as a subtitute has helped to save the whale from extinction. Traditional medicinal uses include treatment of cancer and kidney disorders.

Brunsfelsia americana

Family: *Solanaceae*

A species originating from the West Indies, *Brunsfelsia americana* is known as «lady of the night» because of its very strong nocturnal scent. The shrub which reaches about 3 m in height requires very sheltered humid conditions and is normally propagated from hardwood cuttings or seeds.

Brunsfelsia calycina

Family: *Solanaceae*

Originating from Brazil this species is a small, slow growing shrub with violet-blue flowers which turn white on aging. The common name is «yesterday-today-and tomorrow» and the plant is propagated by cuttings. It requires very sheltered, humid conditions.

Cestrum aurantiacum

Family: *Solanaceae*

A brilliant orange-flowered species which comes from Guatemala, this species, the «golden jessamine», is delicately perfumed at night. It flowers throughout the year and also produces very striking white berries. It is a very vigorous grower and is suitable for hedges. It is grown from seed or from cuttings.

Cestrum elegans

Family: *Solanaceae*

A tropical species originating from Mexico, this plant has carmine-red flowers which are produced throughout the year. It is an evergreen downy shrub best propagated by cuttings and prefers sheltered but sunny areas protected from the wind.

Cestrum nocturnum

Family: *Solanaceae*

From the West Indies and Central America the «night jessamine» or «dama de noche» is a common garden shrub in subtropical regions. Its pale greenish-yellow flowers are heavily perfumed at night. The fruits and sap are poisonous but provide an extract which is used as an antispasmodic in the treatment of epilepsy.

Cestrum parquii

Family: *Solanaceae*

The «willow-leaved cestrum» comes from Chile. It is a very vigorous shrub suitable for hedges and screens. The greenish-yellow flowers are produced in large pendent panicles and are strongly perfumed at night. Propagation is by cuttings.

Cyphomandra betacea

Family: *Solanaceae*

Commonly known as the «tree tomato» this species originates from the Andean region of Peru. It is a shrub or small tree grown for its reddish-orange, egg-shaped berries in South America and throughout the Tropics. The fruit with its strange flavour is eaten raw or cooked.

Datura arborea

Family: *Solanaceae*

Datura arborea is a commonly cultivated shrub, known as «angel's trumpet», which originates from Chile and Peru. It has large, white flowers with five distinct points at the tip of the corolla tube. The flowers are very strongly scented especially at night. It is easily propagated by cuttings.

Datura chlorantha

Family: *Solanaceae*

The «yellow datura» or «moonflower» is said to be from South America but its exact origin is not known. It has a heavy perfume and a double-flowered, very deep yellow form is known but is uncommon in cultivation.

Datura suaveolens

Family: *Solanaceae*

«Angel's trumpet», from Brazil, is commonly grown for its large ornamental flowers. The whole plant is poisonous, especially the leaves and flowers because they contain strong narcotics. These have important medicinal value though producing delirium. They are also rich in alkaloids like daturine with similar properties to atropine.

Iochroma cyaneum

Family: *Solanaceae*

Also known as *I. tubulosa* this plant comes from Columbia and is a vigorously growing velvety-leaved shrub reaching about 3 metres. It flowers in Spring and Summer and likes open sunny habitats with regular watering. It is usually propagated from cuttings.

Solandra nitida

Family: *Solanaceae*

This Mexican species is a very vigorous climber whose large yellow flowers justify its common name of «gold cup». It is a very rapidly growing species which requires plenty of space and regular hard pruning as the flowers are formed on the new growth. It is very easily propagated from cuttings.

Solanum jasminoides

Family: *Solanaceae*

A relative of the potato, this vigorous creeper comes from Brazil. Its star-shaped, white flowers borne in large clusters make it especially useful for covering walls and fences. It will grow under most conditions and flowers almost continuously if in shade. Various cultivars are known including a rare variegated-leaved form.

Solanum muricatum

Family: *Solanaceae*

Originally from Peru the «pear-melon» or «egg-plant» is a small shrub grown in Subtropical and warm-temperate areas for its edible fruit which has a slightly astringent, melon-like flavour and can be cooked or eaten raw. It has delicate purple flowers and is usually grown from cuttings.

Solanum wendlandii

Family: *Solanaceae*

This very attractive shrubby climber is originally from Costa Rica. It has prickly stems and large lavender-blue flowers up to 6 cm. across borne in clusters. It prefers very warm, moist conditions and is propagated by means of cuttings. It is commonly called «potato vine».

Streptosolen jamesonii

Family: *Solanaceae*

One of the most decorative of all garden shrubs which produces brilliant orange and yellow flowers throughout the year, it originally comes from Columbia and Ecuador and requires a sunny position and plenty of water. Its brittle branches are easily damaged by wind and it does not grow well in full shade. Propagation is by cuttings. The common name is «marmalade plant».

Brachychiton acerifolium

Family: *Sterculiaceae*

Originating from Australia, this beautiful tree produces an abundance of tiny bright red flowers giving rise to the common name of «flame tree». The leaves are deciduous and often the flowers are produced when the tree is leafless making the display even more spectacular. It is a slow growing tree with tough bark which produces both gum and fibre.

Brachychiton diversifolium

Family: *Sterculiaceae*

The «kurrajong» is an Australian tree with a large, swollen trunk and provides good shade. The Australian Aborigines use the bark for clothing and the leaves for animal food. A useful gum can also be extracted from the trunk. The whitish-red flowers are attractive and the orange seeds are the usual means of propagation.

Dombeya wallichii *(D. X Cayeuxii)*

Family: *Sterculiaceae*

This shrub or small tree is a native of Madagascar and East Africa. It is said by some authorities to be of hybrid origin. It is a very showy plant when in full flower and covered with masses of pink pendulous balls. It is normally grown only as an ornamental though in East Africa the wood is also considered to be useful.

Tamarix pentandra

Family: *Tamaricaceae*

This Mediterranean plant, with its dark, pink flowers is grown both as an ornamental plant and, because of its drought resistance and tolerance of saline conditions, as a soil stabilizer. It is also useful for wind-breaks especially in sandy habitats. The bark is used for tanning and the wood for fuel. Some *Tamarix* species have medicinal properties.

Citharexylum spinosum

Family: *Verbenaceae*

This small, deciduous tree originates from the West Indian Islands. It is commonly known as «bella-sombra» or «fiddlewood» and produces long pendent racemes of very fragant flowers. In autumn the leaves turn from pale green to deep red before falling and the tree can then be pruned hard to stimulate new growth and increase flower production for the next year.

Clerodendron splendens

Family: *Verbenaceae*

A member of a genus of about 300 tropical and subtropical trees, shrubs and climbers, this species is a West and Central African shrub frequently found in subtropical gardens. It is a robust species which can be trained as a climber and is sometimes known as the «glory bower». It is usually propagated from seed and should be regularly watered.

Duranta repens

Family: *Verbenaceae*

The «sky flower» or «pigeon berry» is a Tropical American plant from Florida. West Indies, Mexico and south to Brazil. It is used in gardens as a specimen plant or to form hedges. Both the flowers and fruits are used medicinally though the seeds are poisonous. Infusions of the leaves are also said to be of medicinal value.

Lantana camara

Family: *Verbenaceae*

The «Jamaica mountain sage» is one of the most commonly cultivated subtropical garden plants. It originally comes from Jamaica in the West Indies but has become a serious weed in many parts of the humid Tropics. The black fruited, prickly wild form is easily reproduced from seed but the more attractive modern cultivars are mostly sterile and must be propagated from cuttings.

Petrea volubilis

Family: *Verbenaceae*

A twining, scrambling shrub up to 7 or 8 m with very
ornamental blue-purplish racemes of flowers. Its
home is in Mexico, Central America and the West
Indies and the rough leaves give it the common name
of «sandpaper vine». It is an excellent subject for pergolas or for wall cover and is normally grown from
seed.

Agave americana var. medio-picta

Family: *Agavaceae*

Of Mexican *Agave americana* is commonly known as the «century plant» or «pitera». The variety illustrated, var. *medio-picta,* probably arose in cultivation and is one of the most popular garden succulents. It is propagated from offsets arising from the base of the plant or from bulbils in the inflorescence and grows well in sunny places if regulary watered.

Agave attenuata

Family: *Agavaceae*

This Mexican species is a very desirable garden plant with its large rosettes of bluish leaves and gracefully arching inflorescence of greenish-yellow to white flowers. Older rosettes are borne on a short stem up to one metre and small plants arise from the base and may be taken as cuttings. The inflorescence also occasionally produces bulbils for propagation.

Agave sisalana

Family: *Agavaceae*

The sisal agave or «yaxci» originates from Mexico and the leaves are a major source of the fibre «sisal hemp» which is extremely strong and used for ropes, carpets and sacking. The plant is also a very useful, large subject for landscape gardening in dry, hot regions. It is usually grown from offsets.

Furcraea gigantea

Family: *Agavaceae*

Native to Tropical America this plant is commonly cultivated both as an ornamental in dry, hot areas and for its leaf-fibre which is used for making string, ropes and sacks. It is widely grown commercially in Madagascar, India and Mauritius (the fibre is known as Mauritius hemp) where it is now naturalized. The flowering stems reach up to 12 m and bear bulbils for propagation.

Phormium tenax

Family: *Agavaceae*

The common name «New Zealand flax» or «New Zealand hemp» indicates the country of origin of this species. It was used by the Maoris for fibre and is now grown on a commercial scale in New Zealand, Central Africa, Mauritius and in South America as a source of fibre for string. In many other places it is grown as a very resistant ornamental.

Bomarea multiflora

Family: *Amaryllidaceae*

From Columbia and Venezuela, this attractive climbing plant is very rarely found in cultivation but is of great potential as a subtropical garden plant. In South America the tubers which have a high starch content are eaten locally as a vegetable.

Clivia miniata

Family: *Amaryllidaceae*

A South African species from Natal commonly called the «kafir lily» this plant is a most valuable ornamental. It is usually grown in shady areas, often under trees and produces brilliant orange-red flowers which last well when cut. The plant is propagated by division of the fleshy roots or by seed.

Clivia nobilis

Family: *Amaryllidaceae*

The drooping red flowers with green tips give this species its common name of «greentip kafir lily». It is a native of South Africa and is an excellent garden subject for shady, humid places. Propagation is by means of root division or from seed.

Crinum asiaticum

Family: *Amaryllidaceae*

Widely grown as an ornamental, this species in its native India and Polynesia has numerous medicinal uses. Though poisonous to both Man and animals the plant is used as an emetic and to induce sweating as well as to treat inflammation. It is a shade-loving plant with large bulbs and long, pale green leaves.

Monstera deliciosa

Family: *Araceae*

Commonly known as «cheese plant» or «Mexican bread-fruit» the principal use of this species is as a tough, resistant house-plant. It has, however, an edible cone-shaped fruit with a pineapple flavour which may be eaten raw or pulped to make drinks and ices.

Zantedeschia aethiopica

Family: *Araceae*

The «calla lily» or «lily of the Nile» comes originally from Southern Africa but it is naturalized in Hawaii, New Zealand and other countries. It is used as a commercial cut-flower and is a valuable garden plant especially for damp shady places. The tuberous roots can be used as animal food and have a high starch content.

Ananas comosus

Family: *Bromeliaceae*

The «pineapple» is of unknown origin but probably comes from Brazil or Tropical South America. It has been cultivated for its edible fruit for many years in Hawaii where 70% of the world's canned pineapple is produced. The fruit can also be eaten fresh and gives many other products such as syrup, alcohol and cattle food and the leaves produce fibre.

Bromelia pinguin

Family: *Bromeliaceae*

Commonly known as the «pineapple» or «piñuela» this Central American species is an excellent garden plant for semi-shade areas and for low hedges. The fruits are edible but rather acid, but the juice is used for drinks and for medicinal purposes and the leaves have a local use for fibre production.

Bambusa vulgaris

Family: *Graminae*

This Old World Tropical bamboo is widely grown from Java, Africa and the East Indies to Central and South America. The young shoots can be eaten and the strong stems provide building material, fishing poles and furniture. They are also an important source of long-fibre pulp in paper making. The plant also has many medicinal uses.

Cortaderia selloana

Family: *Graminae*

This species, also known as *Cortaderia argentea* is the «Pampas grass» and comes from the plains of Sourthern South America. Its main use in cultivation is as an ornamental but it is also the basis of a paper-making industry in S. America and the roots are supposed to have medicinal properties. Propagation is by root division.

Agapanthus africanus

Famil: *Liliaceae*

The «blue African lily» or «lily of the Nile» occurs in both blue and white-flowered forms. It originates from the Cape region of South Africa and is extensively grown as an ornamental, shade-loving plant. The roots are of medicinal value and several African tribes use a decoction to help ease the pains of childbirth.

Aloe africana

Family: *Liliaceae*

Usually found in dense, bushy habitats this species can reach up to 4 m tall. It is confined to the Eastern Cape region of South Africa where it is locally common. The plant is usually unbranched and the leaves have spines only on the margins. The inflorescence is erect and the yellow or orange flower-tube curved upwards.

Aloe arborescens

Family: *Liliaceae*

A widely distributed species from the Cape to Zimbabwe and Malawi. This is probably the most frequently cultivated *Aloe*. It is a tall branched shrub up to 3 m with orange-red to scarlet racemes and it grows easily from cuttings. It is often used as a hedge plant in S. Africa and is commonly found as a garden shrub in subtropical and Mediterranean regions.

Aloe concinna

Family: *Liliaceae*

A native of the island of Zanzíbar off the East coast of Africa, *Aloe concinna* is a commonly cultivated species both as a pot and garden subject. It branches readily from the base and has green-white spots on the leaves. As with most *Aloe* species it is usually grown from cuttings.

Aloe ferox

Family: *Liliaceae*

Aloe ferox is a widely distributed species from South Africa where it is found in Cape Province, Lesotho and Natal. It is tolerant of both cold and rather wet (750 mm) conditions and is an excellent garden subject. The leaves may be spiny on both surfaces or have spines only on the margins. The racemes are always erect and the flowers orange to scarlet.

Aloe marlothii

Family: *Liliaceae*

A very robust, single-stemmed species *A. marlothii*, comes from South and South East Africa (Transvaal, Botswana, Swaziland, Natal, Zimbabwe and Moçambique). Very large, old plants may reach 6 m. The leaves are grey-green with a reddish tinge and usually have spines on both surfaces. The distinguishing features of the plant are the horizontally disposed nature of inflorescences and the golden-red flowers.

Aloe mutabilis

Family: *Liliaceae*

A very attractive species with bluish-green leaves *A. mutabilis* is native to the Transvaal district of South Africa. The inflorescences are usually simple and the flower buds scarlet. The open flowers quickly change to yellow or greenish yellow hence the name *mutabilis*. This species, uncommon in cultivation, is a very desirable garden plant.

Aloe ortholopha

Family: *Liliaceae*

A stemless, unbranched plant, *A. ortholopha* comes only from Zimbabwe and Zambia where it is found on rocky, treeless hillsides in dry areas. The leaves are grey-green with a very strong pinkish tinge and the leaf-margins are strongly toothed. The horizontal racemes of attractive blood-red flowers are almost 35 cm long.

Aloe striatula

Family: *Liliaceae*

This low, branching shrub is from the Eastern Cape of Good Hope and Lesotho where it is found in dry mountain areas between 1000 and 1500 m. The leaf-sheaths are green-striped, giving the name *striatula* and the buds are green, turning yellow as the flower opens. It is a fairly common, easily grown garden plant in dry areas and can be propagated from cuttings.

Aloe vera

Family: *Liliaceae*

This widely cultivated, yellow-flowered *Aloe,* is of unknown origin. It is considered by some to be Mediterranean but others assign it to S. Arabia or even to the Canary Islands or Cape Verde. It is the main source of medicinal «aloes» which is used for a wide variety of treatments including worms, as a cathartic and in the treatment of skin burns.

Gloriosa rothschildiana

Family: *Liliaceae*

The «glory lily» is a climbing plant from Tropical Africa and Asia. It is a valuable ornamental but has a long tradition of use as a medicinal plant. It is used to treat parasitic worms and leprosy and contains many alkaloids including colchicine which is applied to supress gout. The seeds may have anti-cancer properties.

Yucca eliphantipes

Family: *Liliaceae*

One of the largest *Yucca* species reaching over 15 m in height, *Y. eliphantipes* is a very important garden plant. It originates from Guatemala and Mexico, is very decorative and can be grown in large pots as an indoor or patio plant. It is usually propagated by cuttings from older plants which branch after flowering.

Heliconia humilis

Family: *Musaceae*

This species, whose leaves are used for thatching in its native South America, is usually grown as an ornamental and commercially, on a limited scale, for cut-flowers. The plant, known as lobster claw or simply Heliconia requires a warm, humid site and rich soil for successful cultivation and is propagated from seed or by division.

Musa acuminata

Family: *Musaceae*

This species is the main source of edible bananas and has played a major rôle in the extensive hybridisation and selection leading to the modern cultivars, including the «dwarf cavendish» Apart from the food value of the fruits, the stems and leaves are used for forage and some forms are an important source of acaba fibre and Manila hemp.

Musa acuminata «Giant Cavendish»

Family: *Musaceae*

The West Indian or «giant cavendish banana» is one of the most important banana cultivars. It is taller and more slender than the «dwarf cavendish» and the fruit is less sweet. It is widely cultivated in the West Indies and Central America but is not suitable for windy conditions. The fruit crop is of considerable economic importance in these countries.

Ravenala madagascariensis

Family: *Musaceae*

The well-known «traveller's tree» with its distinctive fan-like leaf arrangement comes from the Indian Ocean island of Madagascar. The swollen boat-shaped bases of the petioles hold a reserve of water which can be used as drinking-water in an emergency thus giving the plant its common name. It is frequently seen in subtropical parks and gardens as an ornamental and is propagated from seed.

Strelitzia nicolaei

Family: *Musaceae*

This species is commonly known as the «great white strelitzia». It is a robust plant of up to 4 m and developes a trunk. The banana-like leaves grow in a single plane and the white flowers are spectacular. The plant is grow from seed or by division and requires a sheltered humid environment.

Strelitzia reginae

Family: *Musaceae*

The «strelitzia» or «bird of paradise flower» is from South Africa and Transkei. It is widely cultivated both for ornamental purposes and as a long-lasting cut flower. It is a slow-growing plant which requires about seven years to flower from seed. For commercial purposes it is usually reproduced by division of the rootstock.

Arecastrum romanzoffianum

Family: *Palmae*

This greyish, smooth-trunked palm comes from the south of Brazil, Bolivia and Argentina and is commonly known as «queen palm». It is a tall species reaching 15 m and, though requiring shade when small, thrives in full sun provided that it is well watered. It is usually propagated from seeds which germinate quickly (30 days) for a palm. It is often found in cultivation under the name *Cocos plumosa.*

Brahea armata

Family: *Palmae*

The «blue hesper palm» comes from the Baja California region of Mexico and is widely cultivated for its attractive bluish foliage and long feathery inflorescences. Though usually seen in gardens as small specimens the trunks can reach about 12 m. It is useful for dry coastal zones as it is very resistant to dry conditions and poor soils. It is a very slow-growing species which is usually propagated by seed.

Chamaerops humilis

Family: *Palmae*

Commonly known as the «palmito» or «European fan palm» this species is Mediterranean in origin and occurs in virtually all the countries bordering the Mediterranean Sea. It is slow-growing species and may form several trunks which eventually can reach up to 3 or 4 m. The foliage is variable in colour from dull green to blue-glaucous and several forms are cultivated. It is usually grown from seed which takes 60-90 days to germinate.

Coccos nucifera

Family: *Palmae*

This Polynesian species, the «coconut palm», is one of the World's most important commercial species and the sole source of income for many small Pacific Ocean islands. Almost all parts of the plant are useful but its main economic product is the white flesh of the fruit which yields 60% coconut oil, widely used in the production of butter substitutes, cosmetics and synthetic rubber. The fruit husk produces a valuable fibre and almost all parts have medicinal value.

Howea forsteriana

Family: *Palmae*

This species is native to the Australasian Lord Howe Island. It is very common in cultivation and usually goes by the name of «kentia» or «sentry palm». It is used as a specimen tree in lawns and often as a pot plant. Propagation is from seed but germination may take at least 12 months and growth is slow. It needs well drained soil and regular watering.

Hyophorbe verschaffeltii

Family: *Palmae*

A rare native of the island of Mauritius sometimes found under the name of *Mascarena verschaffeltii*, the «spindle palm» is also relatively unusual in cultivation but is very attractive. It grows in full sun and is resistant to drought and coastal conditions. It is propagated from seed which takes between 6 months and a year to germinate.

Livistona chinensis

Family: *Palmae*

A very commonly cultivated fan palm this species originates from China and Japan. It is a tall, very slow growing species which can reach about 12 m tall. It is one of the hardiest species of palm and resists low temperatures. Young specimens are best grown in shade but larger plants can be planted in full sun.

Phoenix canariensis

Family: *Palmae*

The «Canary date palm» is a native of the Canary Islands. It is a highly appreciated ornamental palm in many parts of the World and though the fruits are scarcely edible some use is made of almost all parts of the plant and palm syrup is extracted from the tip of the trunk on the island of La Gomera.

Phoenix dactylifera

Family: *Palmae*

The «date palm» is grown throughout the Mediterranean region and especially in Arab countries for its edible fruits. It is said to be originally from Asia Minor but is now found as far away as California where it is an important crop plant. The fruits have a high sugar content and are rich in vitamins, and the seeds are fed to camels. Commercial propagation is by suckers.

Roystonea regia

Family: *Palmae*

The well-known «Cuban royal palm», from the island of Cuba is one of the most magnificent of all palms with its tall, silver-grey trunks and long feather-like leaves. It needs rich soil, regular watering and good light and responds to these conditions with rapid growth. It is reproduced from seeds which take about 3-6 months to germinate.

Trachycarpus fortunei

Family: *Palmae*

Originating from the east and central regions of China the «Chusan» or «Chinese windmill palm» is a commonly cultivated species. Garden specimens are usually 2-3 m tall but the species can reach 12 m. It resists most conditions and can be grown from the coast to cool montane areas. The trunks are typically covered in the dark fibre of old leaf-sheaths. Seeds usually germinate in 1-2 months.

Verschaffeltia splendens

Family: *Palmae*

This unusual palm comes from the Seychelle Islands and is not frequently found in cultivation though it is a very attractive species. It can grow to 25 m and does best in hot, humid conditions. The stilt roots are formed even in young plants and propagation is from fresh seed which germinates slowly.

Washingtonia robusta

Family: *Palmae*

Both this and the closely related *Washingtonia filifera* are known as «priest palm» or «Californian fan palm» and originate from the Southern United States. Locally the Indians use the fruit for food, the leaves for thatching and basket-making and the fibre for cordage. Both species are widely grown as ornamentals in subtropical regions of the World.

Pandanus utilis

Family: *Pandanaceae*

Coming originally from the East Indies and the Australian coast *Pandanus utilis* is known as the «screw-pine» or «pandan». It is a very valuable but extremely slow-growing ornamental tree and as the scientific name implies has many uses in its native land. The fruits are edible and the leaves are used for weaving, basketry, roofing and as a source of fibre.

Cymbidium species and hybrids

Family: *Orchidaceae*

Cymbidium is a genus originally from the cooler parts of Eastern Asia such as China, Japan, India etc. and most modern cultivated types have resulted from elaboration of the cross *C. eburneum X Lowianum* which was first produced in the last years of the 19th century. Many spectacular forms are now available and they are amongst the most popular orchids both as plants and cut flowers. Cymbidiums require cool night temperatures below 20°C in order to initiate flowering.

Epidendrum hybrid «X obrianianum»

Family: *Orchidaceae*

Most common cultivated orchids are complex hybrids often involving up to 5 or 6 species of different genera. This plant is, however, a rather more simple but extremely attractive cross between *Epidendrum evectum* from Colombia and *E. radicans* from Guatamala. It is often found under the common names of «baby orchid» or «fire reed orchid».

Odontoglossum crispum hybrids

Family: *Orchidaceae*

Odontoglossum crispum, from the Colombian Andes has made a major contribution to orchid breeding as one of the most important parent species for *Odontoglossum, Odontocidium* and *Odontioda* hybrids. It is a spectacular plant which requires relatively cool, moist conditions. The illustrated plant is one of the many hybrid cultivars.

Paphiopedilum insigne hybrids

Family: *Orchidaceae*

Native to the Himalayan region, *P. insigne* (slipper orchid) was first introduced to cultivation early last century. It has since become one of the main sources of hybrids and cultivars in *Paphiopedilum*. Propagation of this terrestrial species and its hybrids is usually by seed or meristem culture. Requirements vary from temperate conditions to, in the case of some of the Indian species, subtropical (about 30°C and 60% humidity).

Phalaenopsis hybrids

Family: *Orchidaceae*

The «moth orchids» *(Phalaenopsis* species) come from the Far East, especially Phillipines, Borneo, New Guinea and Thailand. Most modern cultivated forms are hybrids originally involving *P. amabilis* from Java. They require warm, shady conditions and a moist environment and are amongst the most attractive of all the modern cultivated orchids.

Alpinia speciosa

Family: *Zingiberaceae*

A South East Asian species this plant is known as «shell ginger» or «porcelain lily». It is an excellent ornamental which is also used in China and Japan as a source of fibre and for paper-making. It is normally propagated by root-division.

Casuarina equisetifolia

Family: *Casuarinaceae*

The «iron wood» or «horsetail tree» is a native of Australia and the Pacific Islands. It is an important cultivated tree because of its extreme drought resistance and value as a wind-break. The wood is extremely strong and heavy and makes excellent fence posts. The bark is used for tanning leather and in folk medicine.

Cycas revoluta

Family: *Cycadaceae*

Coming from China and Japan the «sago palm» is a very useful ornamental palm-like shrub or small tree. The trunk is a source of starch (sago) and the seed is ground into flour and eaten in the Philippines in times of famine. Commercial gum is obtained from the trunk and leaves.